I0008299

Table of Contents

page = page+1 # 2

My Journey

I would have laughed if you had told me a few years ago that I'd be writing a book about coding. Back then, coding felt like secret language spoken only by my parents and teachers. I wasn't one of them. Or at least, that's what I thought.

I remember the first time I tried to write code. I stared at a blank screen, a blinking cursor mocking me, daring me to figure it out. My first program took way longer than I'd like to admit, and when I finally got it to work, I felt like I had just cracked some hieroglyphics. That tiny success was all it took, and I was hooked.

But not everyone around me felt the same way. I saw so many people in my school scared to even try coding. They thought it was only for geniuses or people naturally good at math. Some even avoided it altogether, believing it was too hard or just plain boring. I couldn't blame them—I had those same thoughts once. But the truth is, coding isn't about being born intelligent; it's about curiosity.

One of the moments that meant the most to me was helping my younger sister get into coding. At first, she was like the rest of the people in school; she thought it was just another subject. So, instead of explaining just concepts, I showed her how coding can be a fun experience as well. I helped her write small games, and she loved seeing her code come to life. Watching her go from hesitant to excited made me realize that coding isn't just about tech problems – it can be for fun too!

I know school life can be overwhelming. The constant pressure of grades, tests, and figuring out the future can be a lot for people. Coding became my escape. It wasn't just about learning something useful—it was my way of creating, experimenting, and finding

page = page+1 # 4

a sense of control when everything else felt chaotic. Every time I solved a complex problem; it gave me a rush of accomplishment that few things could.

One of my most significant milestones was competing in the USACO (USA Computing Olympiad). At first, the problems seemed impossible. I'd stare at the screen, re-read the problem statement, and wonder if I was even looking at English. But over time, I learned to break problems into smaller parts, test edge cases, and optimize my solutions. When I finally reached the gold division, I felt like the time spent paid off.

Another turning point was becoming an intern in a software company. At first, I was terrified. What if my code wasn't good enough? What if I messed something up? However, the team welcomed me, and I quickly learned that real-world coding is all about collaboration. Reviewing other people's code and getting feedback on mine taught me more than any tutorial ever could.

Then came the passion projects. Building something from scratch, whether a small web app or an AI-powered tool, made me realize that coding isn't just about algorithms and syntax—it's about creating things that matter. I started using AI tools to speed up my everyday activities, learning how to integrate machine learning into my projects.

Looking back, I realize that coding isn't about memorizing syntax or learning every possible programming language. It's about problem-solving, creativity, and persistence. And if I, a kid who once thought coding was only for geniuses, could get here, so can you. So, if you're just starting, don't be intimidated. Keep learning, keep experimenting, and most importantly, keep coding. Who knows? Maybe one day, you'll be writing your own story too.

Introduction

I'm going to be honest; I have no idea how to start this book, but I do know that it isn't going to be like any educational textbook that you might have bought for school. However, this is still a coding book, which means there will be information given to you that you should keep and learn from. Coding is nothing but giving instructions.

Imagine this: your parents just left on a date night and left you to take care of your younger sibling. Fast forward a couple of hours, and you're playing Fortnite with your friends when, all of a sudden, you get a text. Oh no! You and your sibling have to clean up before your parents get here; otherwise, the night might take a turn for the worse. You run to your sibling and realize they've made a huge mess. How will you tell them to clean up? Well, since they are young, you must give explicit instructions for them to clean up properly. For example, first, you might ask them to clean up their toys, but if you only say that, they will ask you a barrage of questions.

1. First, they might say that they don't want to clean up, but let's move on from that.
2. How can I collect all the toys?
3. Where do I put them?
4. What if they are too heavy?
5. What if I cannot find all of them?

If you can imagine further, your sibling would probably ask even more questions, but for now, let's assume that they cleaned up all the toys in time. Now, you can add to this, for example, by telling them to clean the rest of the room. This might include making their bed, putting away snacks, etc. Like this scenario, in code, you can keep building and adding onto instructions, eventually creating a coding masterpiece.

Coding is also kind of like building complex things with basic shapes, kind of like Legos. At some point in time, you've probably just sat down and built huge buildings with Legos. You've also probably, with the exact same pieces, built something completely different. The image above shows a description of this. The Lego pieces (shapes) are the same, yet you have made two different structures. In the same way, when you code, you use **keywords** that can make a variety of cool programs and projects.

Earlier, I said that code is just a language that the computer understands, and like the real world, there are hundreds and even thousands of languages. In my opinion, the first language a young coder should learn is Python because it's a great language for beginners and is very similar to how a human would give instructions. This book has four parts, and it is divided into four skill levels (rookie, pro, expert, and GOAT), each having some number of programs that increase in difficulty. All in all, there are about 20 programs that can be used in your daily life, be it silly or serious, and all of them are written in Python. Additionally, each program includes details on how I made them, how you can make them, and how to use them.

This book is going to be very different from your average coding textbook. Of course, like any other author, I want you guys to learn, but I have a unique approach. Since this unique approach isn't exactly straightforward, I'll explain how I want you to properly read this book so you can get the most out of this experience!

Like I said before, this book will be problem-based, with each part being split into sections for each program. When starting to read a new program section, it is important to have your PyCharm open, as you should be coded alongside me. Not only that but in another tab, you should have my GitHub open, as it has the working code for all programs, including detailed comments: https://github.com/aryanpoduri2008/GOAT_Coders. When reading each program and the entire book in general, you will stumble across words that you might not understand. Most of the time, these words will be **bolded**, and this means that they are words that you should know. If you don't know the meaning, you can either look at the end of this book for a description or have a dictionary ready with you. The last part of the program is the FOR-GOATs section, where I will give different add-ons. You can try to implement each program on your own time.

Getting Started

Before diving right into code and the funny programs that we'll be creating, I want to talk to you about my sponsor... (just kidding, this isn't a YouTube video). But seriously, before starting to code, you need to have a few things: 1. Computer 2. Curiosity 3. Composure.

If you already have a personal computer, don't worry about this next part, but if you don't have a personal computer, there are still many ways to code.

1. If your school gives you a computer to take home, you can use the website repl.it
2. If your school doesn't give you a computer, ask your parents to use their personal computer(s).
3. If your parents don't have a computer or if they can't give you one, go to a nearby public library, get a card if you need one, hop on a computer, and use the website repl.it

Anyway, I don't know about you, but I just can't help but daze off when doing this part; it's so boring! But I'll try to get through it so you can start coding.

After you have gotten access to a computer, the next step is to download PyCharm. It is a free app that gives you an easy way to code in Python. I recommend checking on the PyCharm website at this link: https://www.jetbrains.com/help/pycharm/getting-started.html for more information.

Keywords: Your First Code!

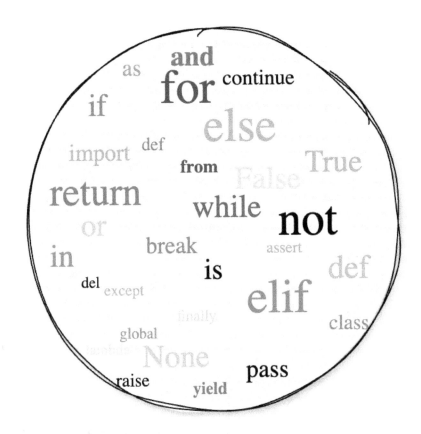

In Python (and in any other language), there are different keywords that can do different actions. Throughout every program that you will make in your life, there are some basic words that you will use and need to know.

Print Statements

The first keyword to know is the print statement. Basically, this just tells the computer what to write and output to the coder. You can print pretty much anything and everything, and though it seems very simple (it is), it can be used in cool ways. If you have set up PyCharm correctly, try printing something out.

```
print ("Rookie to GOAT in 100 days!")
```

In coding, **syntax** is very important, and not using it correctly can lead to errors. Errors occur when the computer either can't understand your code (because it's missing the correct punctuation) or when the code is written in a way that prevents it from running properly.

An example of a syntax error where the syntax is wrong can be shown in any language – including English. Take this example here:

Let's eat kids!
Let's eat, kids!

Though the only difference between the two sentences is the comma, the meanings are completely different! The first sentence is probably said by a man-eating giant, while the second is something a caring mother would say. So, in the same way as English, make sure that your syntax is always correct. For print statements, the parentheses and quotes must be put around the text you want to print.

Commenting

This isn't like **print,** as it isn't a keyword, but it is a key topic in coding. Commenting is when a coder writes text surrounding the code they wrote to make it easier for others to understand the code. Otherwise, if lots of code is written, people would have trouble figuring out what the person wrote, and when working as a team, it would waste lots of time. In Python, the syntax for a comment is

```
# whatever you want to say
```

It is important to include the **#** because that is how the computer understands that it is a comment and not part of the actual code. The computer will then skip this comment and go to the next code line. Now, you might be wondering why this is important, and that's because the goal of this book is to become the GOAT coder. Coding, in many ways, is an art, and if we master it to perfection, we can continue to reap rewards. Just imagine not studying for a test, but you walked in and still aced it. That's the type of satisfaction and rewarding experience I'm talking about. When you comment enough and well, your code can be read like poetry.

Variables

Variables in code are like lockers in school. You use a locker to store some items, like books, backpacks, and more, and to open the locker, there is a unique key. In coding, the only difference is that instead of a key, there is a label, and instead of being physical items that it can have, it stores data.

```
points = 5
```

The code above shows how to make a variable. In this case, the data you want to keep in the variable (locker) is the number five, which represents the number of points in a game. The label *points* act as the key to the locker. Keep in mind that variable names cannot have spaces; instead, you can use underscores. You probably don't understand what's so cool in this, but wait, there's more! The main thing is how we can change the data in the variable.

page = page+1 # 12

In a locker, to change the item that is inside, we have to manually open the locker, put in a new thing, and close the locker, which is a waste of time.

```
points = points + 1
```

The line of code above shows how a variable can be changed and updated. In this line, we are first asking the computer to add one to the data stored and put it back into the variable (locker). Since we first initialized *points* to 5, when we add one to it, it will become 6. However, we don't actually have to do the math, and we can simply assume that the computer did the math and updated it correctly.

Now, let's see a simple way we can use a variable, also using the print statements we learned before. Try out this code below in PyCharm.

```
points = 5
print (points)
```

This piece of code looks much harder than it actually is. The first line is just initializing the *points* to 5, and the second line is printing *points*. Now, this is a bit different than printing data, but it is still the same concept. When looking at the print statement, the computer sees that there are no quotes around the text, which tells it that it is supposed to print a variable. (As I said, the syntax is very important!) To print a variable, the computer, rather than printing the label, unlocks the locker and prints the data kept inside, which in this case is 5.

```
points = 5
print ("Total Points:" + points)
```

Another cool thing you can do with both print statements and variables is mix and mash both together. In the code snippet above, I used the + key to add a string and a variable. The + just tells the computer to place the content of points onto the end of the first string. Try it out, and I bet the output will be something like this:

"Total Points: 5"

If this is all hard to understand, don't worry; you will see how great the variables are when we get to the programs that we will be making.

Basic Data Types

This next topic is also not about a specific keyword but is important in coding in any language. Data types are the different data that can be stored in a **variable**. There are many types of data types, and most are the same in all coding languages. These are the basic ones...

- **Strings**
  - This data type stores text.
  - For example, the text "Harry Potter" is called a string and can be stored in a variable, as well as anything enclosed in quotes.
- **Integers**
  - This data type stores whole numbers.
  - These values include small numbers like 3 and large numbers like 13352642, are integers and can be stored in variables.
  - For example, you can use integers to store game scores.

page = page+1 # 14

- Floats
  - This is like integers, but instead of whole numbers, they include decimals.
  - Numbers like 3.1415 and 13352642.1356 are called **floats** or **floating-point integers**. Keep in mind that the key difference between floats and integers is that all whole numbers are integers and cannot be floats.
  - For example, you can use these to store GPAs or sports stats.
- **Booleans**
  - This is by far the simplest data type, as it can either store **True** or **False** values.
  - You can use booleans to store answers to yes-or-no questions. For example, do you like coding? (I promise by the end of this, you will).
- **None** Type
  - The **None** type represents the absence of data. Unlike all the other data types, none just means nothing or no value.
  - For example, if a program asks for a username, but the user did not enter one, the variable will be set to a default **None** value.

Those are the five major data types used throughout any program. Of course, there are many others, but I will introduce you to them as we go on.

Basic Math Operations

Just like in real life, these math operations are very boring yet important. Again, this is pretty obvious since in code, the **+** is add, - is subtract, * is multiply, and / is divide. There are many more characters that do math but these four are the main ones. In coding, we can do math on data types like integers and floats. Go ahead and try out this snippet of code.

```
multiply = 2 * 1
print (multiply)
```

After running this code, you should get 2 as the output. We can take this further by getting the computer to do more complicated math like this.

```
complicated_math = 2 * 1 + 5
print (complicated_math)
```

Now, it isn't really that complicated, but the output should be 7. From this, we can see the power of the computer and how it can do much more complicated math than we can in an instant. The next thing we can do is do math with variables. Try the code below.

```
num1 = 1
num2 = 2
variable_math = num1 + num2
print (variable_math)
```

The computer output should be 1 + 2, which is 3. Again, this is easy math, and anyone can do things like this, so what's so amazing about it? Well, why don't you use huge numbers and try doing things like the above and see if you can come up with the answer before the computer? (No offense, but you'll probably lose). Now, on the off chance you've managed to beat the computer or even come close, I'm sorry to tell you but the computer doesn't even break a sweat with these computations. But if you really want to challenge the computer, you should try this code right here:

```
print ("2 to the power of 1024 is" + 2 ** 1024)
```

If you haven't seen this operator, it just means **2 to the power of 1024**, which is obviously a much harder math problem than what we made the computer do before.

String Operations

Like math operations, you can also do simple and complex things with strings. Refreshing from *Basic Data Types*, we know strings store any words, phrases, and text itself that are enclosed by quotes. But let's look at some operations and functions we can do with them.

- **Concatenation (+):** This is the term for joining two strings together by adding one to the end of the other. For example, take a look at this print statement and its output.

```
book = "GOAT Coders"
print ("Yo, have you read " + book + " book")
```

Feel free to try it out yourself. In fact, we've done something similar when we looked at variables in the previous section. Now, when doing this, it is important to make sure you are using two strings because the computer will get confused many times.

If you were to create a variable like this, the program would error out. This is because the computer cannot add an integer with a string; it can only work with data of the same type.

- **Repetition (*):** When we want to repeat a string several times, we can use the * operator. Take a look at this example and its output.

```
print ("YES!" * 3)
```

As you can see, this is pretty straightforward. We are literally repeating the string "YES" three times and printing it out. When using the * operator to do this, you are actually required to multiply the to-be-repeated string with an integer.

- **Length (len)**: Another important operation of strings is the length. If we have a string, how would we know the length of it? Take a look at this example.

```
num_digits = len("1000000")
```

This comes very handy when we get into looping over strings and delve deeper into programming, it'll become one of the functions you use the most.

- **Conversion to String (str)**: One last operation of strings is converting another data type to string type. For example, you want to print a non-string value, one way to do it is:

```
print ("How many zeroes in 1 million? Is it " + str(num_digits-1) + "?")
```

Concatenation, repetition, and length are the three most important string operations that you must know. All three of them stand as building blocks for all other complex operations. When you become more efficient in coding, you'll learn that there are tens of cool functions that can do their own unique operations and tasks, but for now, this is what you need to know.

Input and Output

To understand **inputs** and **outputs**, let's look at how to calculate GPA from grades. In this case, the inputs are two numbers, and the output is the GPA of the two grades.

Unlike the last few "keywords" we have gone over, this involves a specific keyword and is used in a specific way. Try out the code line below: asking the user for two of their grades and storing them into variables.

```
grade_one = input ("What is your first grade? (Answer from 1 to 4)")
grade_two = input ("What is your second grade? (Answer from 1 to 4)")
```

The **input** keyword, in a way, is just like a **print** since it displays whatever text or question you want. The difference is that the computer stores whatever the user writes in the **console into a variable**. In this example, they will answer with their two grades. But now that we have the user input, how do we output the GPA? To calculate the GPA, we just take the average of the grades.

```
gpa = (grade_one + grade_two ) / 2
print (gpa)
```

After running this code snippet, we see that the computer correctly printed the gpa for the grades that we input. In this way, we can input and output whatever we want and get whatever we need from the user. Inputs can make any program an interactive and fun experience, so why don't you take a bit to play with the **input** function?

Conditional Statements

Conditional statements in code are how the computer makes decisions on what to do. It uses information to find out what the next plan of action is. For example, in real life, you might make decisions like...

- If it is cold, wear a jacket
- If you get a text message, respond
- If your friend tagged you on Instagram, repost it
- If you are done with homework, you watch TV

Different coding languages have different keywords for these conditions, and in Python, the keywords are **if**, **elif**, and **else**.

1. **if** statement: This checks if a certain condition is true or false. If it is true, it executes whatever code is underneath it. Look at the code below.

```python
if school_subject == "math":
    print ("Wow, math? You better ADD fun to your code!")
```

This code snippet is a very simple example of an **if** statement. In this, we want the computer to check if the data stored in the *school_subject* variable is the string "math". Now, keep in mind that for this to work, *school_subject* must be a string (if you don't know what a string is, check *Basic Data Types*). If *school_subject* is equal to "math", then we want to print a funny remark about it. When using conditional statements, it is important that **syntax** and **indentation** are present. Before moving on, try out the code above by creating your own variable and initializing it with different strings like the one below.

```python
school_subject = "math" or school_subject = "science"
```

page = page+1 # 20

See what gets printed in the Python console.

By the way, sorry I didn't tell you about the dad jokes, but be prepared; there's still a bit more coming up.

2. **elif** statement: **elif** statements always follow an **if** statement, and the computer executes the code below when its conditional statement is true and if the previous conditional statements are not true. Building onto the code we built previously, try this.

```python
if school_subject == "math":
    print ("Wow, math? You better ADD fun to your code!")
elif school_subject == "science":
    print ("Science? Your code better be out of this WORLD!")
```

This is pretty straightforward, and the condition works the same as a normal **if**. Now, if you type this:

```python
school_subject = "science"
```

It should print "Science? Your code better be out of this WORLD!" and if you type this:

```python
school_subject = "math"
```

It should still print, "Wow, math? You better ADD fun to your code!".

Another thing about the **elif** statements is the fact that you can use multiple after one another. Again, building upon the previous code, we can see this:

```
if school_subject == "math":
    print ("Wow, math? You better ADD fun to your code!")
elif school_subject == "science":
    print ("Science? Your code better be out of this WORLD!")
elif school_subject == "PE":
    print ("Nice, gym? Your code better be in good SHAPE!")
```

To test this code, similar to the previous two versions, you can create the *school_subject* variable and change the value each time you run the program.

3. **else** statement: **else** statements in Python are like the normal condition. Coders put them at the end of their **ifs** and **elifs**, and the code underneath them is only done when none of the previous conditions are true. Now, to see this in action, put this code at the end of the code we have been working on.

```
else:
    print ("Stop. No other subject is worth a dad joke.")
```

Again, you can change the *school_subject* variable each time you run the program and check the output. Anyways, just so you know, conditional statements are very hard to understand when getting a ton of information at once, so don't worry if you don't get the concepts yet. Throughout the book, I will talk about it more in-depth.

Loops

Loops in code seem very complicated at first, but they are actually not. All they do is repeat some code for as long as you want. Let's say you want to print all numbers from 1 to 23. Based on what we have seen, we would need to type 23 **print** statements.

```
print (1)
print (2)
print (3)
...
```

This is a huge waste of time, and that's where loops are helpful. There are two kinds of loops, each with different keywords and syntax: **for** and **while**.

1. **for** Loop: The **for** loop is used when the coder knows how many times to repeat some action. Imagine this like the Grand Prix. Each driver must race around a track until they reach a set number of laps (the amount differs by the location of the race). To achieve success in the race, the drivers must do specific operations, techniques, and turns correctly for each lap.

   Thinking on the computational side, a **for** loop gives us a variable that starts from zero, and each time it runs the repeated code, the variable increases by one until some max value that you would give. Using this, we can easily make the above problem much simpler. Try this code below that prints numbers from 1 to 23.

   ```
   for num in range (1, 24):
       print (num)
   ```

   At first look, there is a lot going on in this snippet, but let's try to understand it. First, the variable I was talking about is *num*, though it can be named anything you want. Next, we want numbers to start at 1 and end at 23. Now, you might be asking why I wrote 24. This is because the computer repeats until *num* reaches 24, and when it does, it stops the loop. Essentially, the range includes the first number but excludes the second. Looking inside the loop, we are printing our variable *num*, and thanks to the loop, it adds one to each **iteration.**

Wow, that was a lot to get through, but when you run this, it should print the numbers 1 to 23. Again, if you are having any problems, check the syntax and indentation, and feel free to just copy and paste the code.

2. **while** Loop: Unlike **for** loops, in **while** loops, the coder usually doesn't know how many times to repeat the action. In a similar way, you can think of these loops like the 24 Hours of Le Mans. If you don't know, this race ends with a time limit, not by the number of laps. The unique thing about this is that nobody knows how many laps the race will end with. Similarly, a **while** loop only ends when a certain condition is not met or becomes false. Take a look at the code below.

```
num = 1
while num < 24:
    print (num)
    num = num + 1
```

Again, unlike **for** loops, if you do want a variable that increases by one every interaction, you would have to make one and write the code that increases it, as seen in the first and last lines. The condition in this case is *num < 24*, and the loop will only run when this is true, which also means that it will end when the condition is false, which in this case is when *num* equals 24. This code should print the exact same thing as the **for** loop we talked about before.

Loops are what makes a computer superhuman. In fact, you think of your computer as Bruce Banner, and running loops turn him into the Hulk. But... It's not all sunshine and rainbows; they can also make the most powerful person feel stuck.

```
number = 1
while number < 24:
    print (number)
```

Notice the problem with this code. By taking out the incrementing of number, there is no way for the loop to end! (If you want to break this, you can press CMD+C for Mac or CTRL+C for Windows).

Lists

The last thing you need to take from this brief intro is the list. Other than the data types we learned about before, this is probably going to be your most used complex data type as you move on as a programmer. Well, what is a **list**? In Python, a list is just a collection of values stored in a variable in a sequential order. You can think of a list like a train with some amount of train cars. The train cars are in a fixed, sequential order, and they can store anything you want: passengers, coal, food, mail, and more.

```
train = ["passengers", "coal", food", mail"]
```

To initialize a list, you must put every list item (train car) in square brackets like the code above. Currently, *train* has four items in it, displaying the content of each item. Though

page = page+1 # 25

our list only has strings, a list item can contain whatever datatype you want. Now that we have the list, how do we actually access the content within? This is where indexing comes into play. In Python, a list is structured in such a way that each list item has an assigned index.

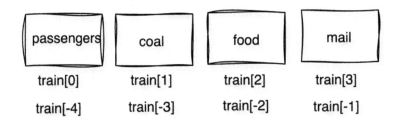

In the diagram, we can see that each list value is mapped to a particular index number. You also probably have noticed that the index starts at zero and not one, and this is very important to remember. In coding and computers, numbers start from zero, and as you keep adding values to the list, the index number goes up. In our example list, passengers are in index zero, coal is in index one, and so on and so forth. In Python, you can also index from the last element of the list by using negative numbers. If you look at the diagram again, the last element starts at 1, then 2, 3, etc. An interesting thing about this is that the same indexing logic works for **strings,** too, using the exact same code. To practice this, run the code below.

```
for i in range(4):
    print ("car " + str(i+1) + " has " + train[i])
```

In this code snippet, the square brackets tell the computer that we are indexing from the list and we are displaying the value of the item in that index. You can also use indexing to change values in the list. Let's say our train stops at a station and replaces the second car with oil instead of coal. Our list will now need a change at the first index (remember, the index starts at zero).

```
train[1] = "oil"
```

The code above will change the item at index one to the string: "oil". The next thing to know when building and working with lists is how to add and remove items. Well, lucky for you, there are many easy ways to do this.

- **append()**: We use this function to add an item to a list. Take a look at the code below.

  ```
  train.append("grass")
  ```

  In this, we are adding an item to the list, and keep in mind that the **append** function can only add an item to the **end** of the list and not anywhere else. So, now *train[4]* points to "grass"

- **insert()**: Now, what if you wanted to add an item in the middle of the list? Well, then, you can use the **insert** function. For this, I recommend you try out a couple of inserts in the list before moving on, so here is an example for you to insert "grains" at index 1 and "metals" at index 3.

  ```
  train.insert("grains", 1)
  train.insert("metals", 3)
  ```

Unlike the append function, you not only have to give the new item but the index in which you want to place it. If you take a look at the before and after of the list, you can see the new item gets placed in that index, and the rest gets pushed back by one index.

- **remove()**: The remove function deletes an item from the list. Run this code below and try to figure out how it works.

```
train.remove("oil")
```

Essentially, the remove function takes a specific value. The computer then looks for the value in the list, and as soon as it sees it, that value gets deleted, and the rest gets pulled forward one index. It's also important to know that it removes the first occurrence of the value in the list.

The final thing to know when dealing with lists is how to loop over them. Just like how we looped over numbers, we can also loop over items in a list – just in a different way. Take a look and run the code below.

```
for car in train:
    print (car)
```

In this code, we are looping over the train list and printing out the values. As you can see, the difference is the range is not there, and that's because we don't need one. Again, strings and lists are similar not only in their indexing but also in looping. You can actually do the exact same code to loop through a string because, in Python, a string is almost like a list of characters. Just instead of looping list item by list item, you loop character by character.

<u>**Review:**</u>

In this section, we learnt basics of Python Language:

- Keywords

- Print statement

- Comments in Python

- Variables

- Basic data types

- Common Math operations

- String operations

- Inputs and Outputs

- Conditional statements

- Looping: For and While

- Overview of Lists

- List operations

Putting It All Together: Your First Program!

Okay, it would be a bit too much to make you write a whole program by yourselves, so I have created one for you. Basically, this program asks you how long your homework will take and then gives you a funny response based on the time you enter. I know, I know, it isn't a useful program but bear with me for now; it has a lot of the things you'll need for the future programs we do.

Before getting into the program, I want to talk a bit more about **while** loops. I've told you that the condition of a **while** loop can look something like this:

```
while number < 23:
```

But you probably weren't thinking that the condition can look like this:

```
while True:
```

While True means run the loop forever unless you hit a break. Imagine this as you keep driving until you run out of gas or something is in your way to force you to stop. For now, take a look at this program:

```
while True:
    homework_time = int (input ("How long will your homework take in
minutes? "))
    if homework_time < 30:
        print ("I don't see any work. I'm asking for your homework. You
know...from school.")
    elif 30 <= homework_time < 60:
        print ("Okay, honestly, you could do this in about 15 minutes if
you tried.")
    elif 60 <= homework_time < 90:
        print ("I mean, it could be worse. Just finish up, and you'll
have time to watch TV.")
    else:
        print ("Holy moly, does your teacher not like you?")

    continue_choice = input ("Do you still have homework? (y/n): ")
    if continue_choice != "y":
        print ("Thanks! Goodbye.")
        break
```

Since this is your first real program and not some code snippet, I'll take you through it line by line... And no, for future programs, I am NOT going to do this; it takes way too much time.

The first line is **while True**, and we just talked about this. The next line is the user input; it's how the computer gets the amount of homework. The keyword **input()**, as we know, takes your input as a string and stores it in a variable. If the string is a number, we can wrap it around with an **int()** to officially make the data an integer. However, if the input isn't a number, it will give an error, so be careful when using it.

So now that we have the input, that is, time to complete the homework, we can start checking which bucket it falls under by using the **if-elif-else** conditional statements. These statements check the time and print different sentences based on their value. If it's under 30 minutes, it prints a funny message. For 30-60 and 60-90 minutes, it prints category-specific statements. If the time exceeds 90 minutes, it prints, "*Holy moly, does your teacher not like you?*"

The next component is the input to ask whether the user has more homework or if it can be used as a check-up when you have finished part of the homework. For this input, we don't need to convert it into an integer because we want to check if the user says "y" or "*n*".

The final part of the program is the final condition to either continue the program and while loop or not. We do this by using another **if** condition.

```
if continue_choice != "y":
    print ("Thanks! Goodbye.")
    break
```

page = page+1 # 31

The response we got in the continue input is stored in the *continue_choice* variable. If it's "y," the program repeats the loop. If it's "n," the program will print "Thanks! *Goodbye.*"... But wait! You must remember to add a **break** statement because if not, the **while** loop will keep going forever.

And now's a great time to talk about why we use **while True?** This has to do with the **scope** of the variable that we are using in the condition *continue_choice*.

Each variable has a different scope, which is the place where a variable can be used and changed. There are two rules for this in Python. When you create a variable,

1. You can use it in any code that appears after the line where it was first defined.
2. It cannot be used in any code that comes after the loop or outside the indentation that it was created in.

If we take a look at the diagram above, we can see in more detail how the scope of a variable changes how it is used. The scope of continue_choice is only inside the while loop, meaning that it cannot be used in the condition since it is outside. Because of this, we have to write the condition inside the loop and put the first condition as True.

Holy cow, that was a lot of information, but hopefully, you now understand how this program works and can try it out on your own.

Review:

A fun program to practice what we learnt in the previous section:

- **if-else-elif** conditions

- Inputs and outputs

- Different ways of using **while** loop

- Converting string to int

Part 1: Our Journey Begins

001: ROOKIE

Every Python journey starts with a computer, a person, and, of course, an idea. The only problem is, how in the world can you program your idea when you've learned Python for around an hour? Well, that's where this book comes in. Eventually, I want you all to be great coders and GOAT coders, but little steps are needed. In this section, I'll help you get through the more unique and detailed code, I'll help you learn new things to do, and most importantly, I'll teach you how to properly make a program that WORKS!

In this part, I will teach you guys how to use string types to your advantage, as well as tell you how to use a random generator in programs. However, the most important thing I will be telling you about is the dictionary. A dictionary is somewhat like a real dictionary, where you find meaning for a given word… but more on that later.

Before we dive in, though, I will tell you that the more you read and the more programs you do in this book, the more useful, funny, and cool the programs will be. With the same logic, these programs in this part will be nothing compared to the programs in the next parts, but they are still funny and silly. In fact, they could be much more tuned to your liking if you start customizing the programs to what you like, and that…is when you'll become a **true programmer!**

Magic 8 Ball

For those who don't know what a magic 8 ball is, it's basically a simple fortune teller. You just ask a question, shake the ball, and then it'll give you different responses, such as...

- It is certain
- It is decidedly so
- Ask again later
- Concentrate and ask again
- Don't count on it
- Very doubtful

Unfortunately, we aren't dealing with Harry Houdini, so I don't think the computer has any magic ability. I guess we'll just have to resort to answering randomly (how sad). But how do we randomly decide out of a list of options? Before looking at that, I want you to meet one of my good buddies!

page = page+1 # 36

<u>Meet Libraries.</u>

No, not the libraries where you read books and play video games on the computers. I'm talking about coding libraries. Coding libraries are like libraries; instead of having books, they have many functions we can use. Woah, woah, woah... back it up. You're probably thinking: *What in the world is a function?* Well, think of a function like a black box. We give it some information, such as variables, lists, or anything, and in return, it outputs some data. Look at the diagram below, and guess what you think the black box (function) does.

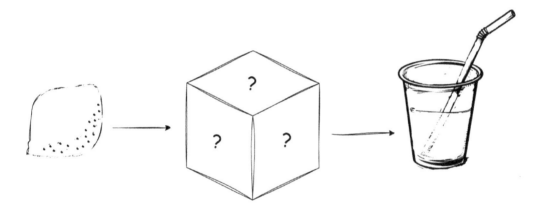

Again, you probably don't understand it, but I'll explain later when we have to make some. Anyways, there are libraries and functions for anything, and actually, you probably didn't notice, but I already introduced them! How's that possible? Well, all the operations on strings and lists, **append**(), **remove**(), and **len**(), are all functions. These functions are in a default library, which is already downloaded when you create a program. Now, coming back to answer our original question on how we randomly decide...I want you to meet my other buddy: **random**.

random is a Python library that will help provide the magic we need. In Python, whenever we want to use the libraries, we use a separate instruction that helps import the library into the Python program:

```
import random
```

The main part is that you must **import** whatever library you want to use in your program. Think of importing is like getting a book from your city library. If you get an error of some sort, it's probably because you typed the library name wrong (believe me, it happens; some of these names are really weird). The next thing you need to know is how we use these library functions.

Now that we can use **random** in our program, let's look at what it can do! Before getting into everything this incredible library can do for us, I just want to say that there could be many functions in each library, but for **random** I'll only be showing you the most important ones.

1. **randint**: This function takes two numbers and gives us a random number between them. If we were trying to get a random number between 1 and 100, we would type this:

```
random.randint(1, 100)
```

The first number is the lowest, the second number is the highest, and ta-da! We will get a number between both numbers.

2. **choice:** This function differs from **randint** because it doesn't deal with numbers. Instead, it takes a list of options and selects a random one. For example, let's say that we have a list called *vacation_list* that has many vacation places to go to, and you want to select a random one:

```
random.choice(vacation_list)
```

The only parameter we give is the list of options, and the next thing you know, we're off on a plane to paradise.

3. **shuffle:** This function takes a list just like choice, but instead of randomly selecting one option, it randomly shuffles it just like how you would with a deck of cards. Let's say that you were making a card game, had a list with all the cards of a deck, and named it... I don't know, probably *cards*. Then, to shuffle the cards just as a dealer would do in any card game, you could do this:

```
random.shuffle(cards)
```

Then, you would get a new list with all the cards shuffled and move on to another part of the program.

As I said before, you can do many more things with this library and basically all the other libraries, too, but these are the three main functions we will use. Anyways, back to our problem of selecting a magic 8-ball response randomly. Out of the three functions I have just talked about, what do you think we should use? I'll give you until the end of the page to think about it.

Have you thought of your answer yet? You probably want the solution now… but too bad! I know some of you just skipped to the bottom of the page without trying. For those who actually thought about it—sorry, but you'll have to wait because of them. For those who didn't even attempt an answer, here's the question again: Out of the three functions we discussed, which one should we use?

Alright, did most of you give it a shot? Great! And for the ones who still didn't… well, you're lucky I can't withhold the answer anymore. But I do appreciate those who tried! After all, isn't it better for 100 guilty people to escape than for one innocent person to suffer? Maybe that's a stretch, but you get the idea. The answer should be obvious—we use **random.choice**() to select a random response from a list!

So... the next thing we should do is create a list of responses we want to choose randomly. To do this, all we do is create a list that has the responses that we talked about at the start of this program:

- It is certain
- It is decidedly so
- Ask again later
- Concentrate and ask again
- Don't count on it
- Very doubtful

Now, you don't have to use these exact responses; if you want, you can add more, remove some, or change them; it's all up to you! To be simple, though, I will be using these six. If you don't know or forgot how to create a list, just go to the previous chapter, where you can learn the correct way to initialize it. Also, if I were you, I would try adding some of my twists to each program. For example, I would use these options for my magic ball:

- Yes, if the sky is blue.
- No, If it's raining.
- How would I know? After all, I'm a computer!
- My brain is fried! Recharge me!
- Ask your Mom!
- I'm sorry, it ain't happening!

Anyhow, after creating the list of responses, we need to get the question from the user. Fortunately, I've already given you all the information you need to do this (Again, I would advise you to look at the previous chapter to learn about inputs!).

After getting the question and storing it in a variable, the final step is to select a random answer. To do this, try the following:

```
answer = random.choice(responses)
```

Note that I named my variable to hold the list of responses as *responses*, so if you are calling it a different name, make sure to change that. Now, all you have to do to finalize the program is print out the randomly selected answer. Voila! Your coded magic 8-ball is a reality!

But before moving on to our next program, keep in mind that there are solutions at the end of this book for all the programs I will teach. However, all silliness aside, I really want all of you to try coding and creating these programs before looking at the solution. That way, you guys are actually learning while having fun. Alright, back to coding paradise!

Review:

- Libraries/Modules
- Functions
- Python module: random

For GOATs: Expand Magic 8-ball with,
1. Provide different modes: classic, sarcastic and philosophical.
2. Keep track of previous answers so you don't repeat them.
3. Introduce a weighted choice to bias a few answers.

Rock Paper Scissors

What was everyone's favorite game back in first grade? Rock-paper-scissors. Even now, people still play it, though mostly for tie-breakers. But let's be honest—sometimes you don't have a friend to play with. But thanks to coding, I'm sure that'll never be a problem again!

In rock-paper-scissors, you have to choose one of the three options to beat your friend, and for you, this might require strategy because of all the things you know and have seen your friend do. Unfortunately, in basic coding, a computer can't think like us and have these complex strategies based on its opponent, but it does have its buddy random. So yes,

I know, we're going to have to suck the fun out of it just like how we did with the Magic 8 ball, but the computer will still feel like a friend in this game.

Before digging into this problem, let's outline how the code will work...

1. Get the user's choice (rock, paper, or scissors)
2. Randomly select the computer's choice
3. Print both selections (player and computer)
4. Figure out who beats whom
5. Print the winner

The first step is simple, especially since we've done it before. How do we get the user's choice and store it in a variable? (The hint is **input**!)

The next step is to select the computer's choice randomly, and we can do that similarly to the Magic 8 ball program. After you've thought about it yourself, here is how I would do it:

```
computer_choice = random.choice(choices)
```

This assumes that the list containing the three options, *rock, paper, and scissors,* is named *choices.* Your variable can be named anything, but make sure to use that variable name instead. Do not forget to **import** the random library. Remember that, in Python, any library that is used must be imported, just like you have to travel to your library before you borrow a book. Otherwise, the program will have an error.

The third step is to print what the player and computer chose. Now, we can obviously just print both choices; however, as you will learn, it isn't as descriptive to the user, and most of the time, when printing information, it is done with a combination of straight-up text and variables. In this case, it would be better to print something like:

"You chose rock."
"I chose paper."

There are two main ways to print text and variables.

1. **Addition (+):** In this technique, to combine a string and a variable, all you do is type a + in between. For example, in our case, we could do something like this:

   ```
   print ("You chose "+ player_choice)
   print ("I chose "+ computer_choice)
   ```

   The above code would print out what we want. The main thing with this is that we have to make sure that the variable we are using is of the **string** data type, and if it isn't, we have to convert it using **str()** function. Otherwise, the computer will give you lots of messy errors.

2. **f-strings:** Unlike regular strings, **f-strings** have a feature that helps coders use variables inside of their strings. To start an **f-string,** just type an **f** in front of the string, and to tell the computer what is a variable and what isn't, you need to enclose all your variables in curly brackets. You can also do the same print statements above like this:

```
print (f "You chose {player_choice} ")
print (f "I chose {computer_choice} ")
```

In general, this technique is used more because users don't have to worry about the errors that come when the variable is not a string type, and it is also very simple once you get the hang of it. For this reason, throughout the book, whenever we come across a situation where we have to print a string with variables, we'll use the **f-strings**.

Getting back to this step, try using **f-strings** to make the output and print statements of both selections more descriptive. It doesn't have to say the same thing as mine but feel free to use it.

The next step is a bit tricky since it's the first thing in this program that uses an entirely new way of thinking. Unlike the magic 8 ball, we can't just print both choices; we must find the winner. In rock-paper-scissors, *paper beats rock; scissors beat paper, and rock beats scissors*. To code this, there is a specific way to check whether user and computer choices align with these scenarios.

The way I'm talking about it is, of course, using **if** conditions. To see this, first, let's look at all possible combinations that could happen.

Rock + Scissors	Scissors + Paper	Paper + Rock
Rock + Paper	Scissors + Rock	Paper + Scissors
Rock + Rock	Scissors + Scissors	Paper + Paper

Each scenario is *player_choice + computer_choice*. The first row shows when the player wins, the second row is when the computer wins, and the last row is when it is a tie. Out of the nine scenarios, there are three groups of three, each having different outcomes. Obviously, if the computer and player choose the same option, it will be a tie. Now that we know this, all we have to do is put it in code, and wherever three different results need different outputs, well, we use... **if** conditions!

The first condition that we can code is if it is a tie. It's straightforward, but here is the code:

```
if player_choice == computer_choice:
    print ("Wow, it's a tie!?")
```

We've already done these **if** conditions in the last part, but all this does is check if the *player_choice* is equal to the *computer_choice*. If it is equal, it prints that it is a tie. The following condition is a bit complicated. We want a condition that fits all three scenarios in which the player wins and then prints a message saying that the player won.

Before examining our condition, let's discuss the different keywords used when making conditions like these.

1. **and**: The and keyword is just like it seems. Just like in English, you can use the **and** keyword when you want code to run if multiple conditions are met. For example, two football teams are playing a game, and a kicker is about to kick the game-winning field goal. You might say he will only make it if the wind speed is 0 and the field is not wet. To code this, you could type:

```
if wind_speed == 0 and field != "wet":
    print ("Kicker is making it!")
```

Using the **and** keyword makes it so the computer will only print the statement if *wind_speed* equals zero and the *field* is not wet.

2. **or**: The **or** keyword is also just like it seems. Coders use the **or** keyword if they want code to run when at least one condition is matched out of a group. For example, let's say two football teams are playing a game, and two critical players might not play (call them *player1* and *player2*). You might say that the team will win if *player1* plays or *player2* plays, and to code this, you could type:

```
if player1 == True or player2 == True:
    print ("This team will win!")
```

Using the **or** keyword makes it so that the computer will print this statement if either *player1* equals true or *player2* equals true (assuming that *player1* and *player2* will be equal to true if they are playing and false if they are not).

Now that we know these two keywords (**and, or**), making the complex condition for our rock paper scissors problem will be easier. First, let's take one of the scenarios where the

page = page+1 # 49

player wins: the player does *rock,* and the computer does *scissors.* The condition for this would be something like this:

```
if player_choice == "rock" and computer_choice == "scissors":
    print ("Dang it... you win.")
```

As you can see, I use the **and** keyword to make the computer only print the winning statement if the player choice is rock and the computer choice is scissors. Like this, we can add the other two player-win scenarios, this time using the **or** keyword to connect them:

```
if (player_choice == "rock" and computer_choice == "scissors") or
    (player_choice == "scissors" and computer_choice == "paper") or
    (player_choice == "paper" and computer_choice == "rock") :
    print ("Dang it... you win.")
```

When making complex **if** conditions like the above, it is good practice to use parentheses to make the code look neater and it can also make sure the condition works as you want. Though this condition seems pretty complicated, it is actually a straightforward concept.

Now that we have made conditions for six of the nine scenarios in the table above, we have to end the **if** conditions with an **else** statement for the scenarios where the computer wins. Before looking at the code below, it is okay if you don't understand it fully since we'll practice these concepts throughout the book, even when we look into more fun topics. Anyways, here are all the **if** statements.

```
if player_choice == computer_choice:
    print ("Wow, it's a tie!?")
elif (player_choice == "rock" and computer_choice == "scissors") or
    (player_choice == "scissors" and computer_choice == "paper") or
```

```
    (player_choice == "paper" and computer_choice == "rock"):
        print ("Dang it... you win")
else:
        print ("Haha, you lost!")
```

Again, this might seem a bit overwhelming initially, but you can always run through the code yourself, testing things out whenever you don't understand things. I hope you are doing things like that because that will make you a better coder!

Alright, now for the final step... edge cases! Yeah, I know, I didn't mention this in the original plan, but trust me, this is one of those things that can either make you look like a genius or completely ruin your program in the most embarrassing way possible.

Think of coding like making a sandwich. If you only test your sandwich by taking a bite from the middle, you might think, "Wow, this is perfect!" But then, someone else takes a bite from the edge and finds out you forgot to spread the peanut butter all the way. Now, your sandwich (or program) is a mess, and suddenly, your reputation as a sandwich (or coding) expert is on the line.

Edge cases are those weird, unexpected situations where your program might entirely fall apart. Imagine you're coding a calculator app, and it works great—until someone tries to divide by zero. Boom! Instant crash. If you don't test for edge cases, your program might work most of the time, but the one time it doesn't is when your teacher, your friend, or that one annoying kid in class finds a way to break it. And trust me, they will try.

So, always test for the weird stuff. Try ridiculously long inputs, blank inputs, negative numbers, or things that should be impossible. Because if you don't, someone else will—and they won't be as nice about it.

Returning to the rock-paper-scissors program, what happens if the player inputs "Rock" instead of "rock"? You might think that capitalizing the letter "r" won't change anything, but computers are very strict about this. If the computer had also picked "rock" with lowercase "r," it should have been a tie. However, since the player and the computer had chosen the same but with a different case, it would treat both strings differently. Fortunately, there is a simple fix for problems such as these. Meet **lower()** and **upper()**!

1. **Lower()**: This function takes any string and makes every letter in it lowercase. So, if a player inputs "Rock," we could make the r lowercase by doing this.

```
player_choice = player_choice.lower()
```

Feel free to try it out, but it should change the player input into lowercase "r."

2. **Upper()**: This function is just the opposite of the lower function. All it does is take a string and uppercase every letter in it.

```
player_choice = player_choice.upper()
```

This would change the value from "rock" to "ROCK".

So, to solve the edge case, we have to use the **lower** function on the *player_choice* variable before the computer checks the **if** conditions. Again, before going to the next program, there are solutions at the end of the book, so check them out if you get stuck or want to check your program. Anyways, there you go! The rock-paper-scissors program is finally complete!

<u>**Review:**</u>

- Printing mixed types of data using:
  - Addition (+) operation
  - f-strings
- Using logical operations in conditions
- Converting strings to lower or upper case

For GOATs: Expand RPS with five options instead of three, where each one beats the other four. You can also affect the randomness by adding more weight to a particular selection (ex: rock).

English to Pirate

Have you ever watched a pirate movie and wondered why or even how pirates talk so weirdly? I have definitely tried talking like a pirate, though it was much more challenging than I initially thought. Well, no fear, coding is here! (Alright, that was corny) In this program, we'll try to translate a sentence straight into pirate-speak.

Basically, in this program, we'll try to create a table so that each English word corresponds to a pirate word and, from there, translate each word in the input sentence to the pirate version of it. For example, in the table, we could have words like:

- Hello   Ahoy

- Friend   Matey

- Yes   Aye

- No   Nay

- Money   Doubloons

- My   Me

The only problem is that we don't know any data type that can act like a table. Of course, we could use two lists and do something like that, or we can place English word and pirate word next to each other in a single list, which seems a bit complicated.

Fortunately, Python and other coding languages have something called **dictionaries**. A dictionary in Python is a special kind of list where each item has a key and a value. Instead of finding a value through an index (like in a list), we can look the value up with that key. I mean, just look at an actual dictionary. In the dictionary, we find words that we don't know and find their meanings. Python dictionaries act in the same way. Hopefully, you can now see the power of dictionaries and how we can use them in this program to help us correspond English words to their pirate versions.

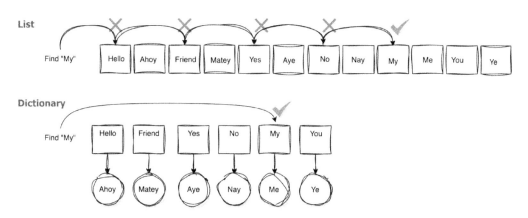

Going into the syntax, here is how to initialize a dictionary in Python.

```
pirate_dict = {
    "hello": "ahoy",
    "friend": "matey",
    "yes": "aye",
    "no": "nay"
}
```

When creating a dictionary, each item starts with the key, then the value is separated by a colon. The main advantage of a dictionary, though, is getting values based on those keys. That is very similar to how a list gets values through an index.

```
pirate_version = pirate_dict["hello"]
```

In the above example, the *priate_version* variable will get the value of "hello" in the pirate dictionary, "ahoy." Try printing *priate_version!* Dictionaries, like all the other data types, have many built-in functions. Of course, I won't be able to review all of them, but here are the important ones.

1. **Keys()**: This function returns a list of all the keys in the dictionary and is mainly used when looping over a dictionary by its keys. So, for the dictionary that we created above -- *pirate_dict* -- the keys function would do this:

   pirate_dict.keys() -> ["hello", "friend", "yes", "no"]

   As you can see, when you use the **keys** function, it lists all the keys you can use to loop over.

2. **values()**: This function is similar to the keys function, but instead, it returns a list of the dictionary's values. It would look something like this for *pirate_dict*:

   pirate_dict.values() -> ["ahoy", "matey", "aye", "nay"]

   Like keys, the **values** function gives a list of values you can use to loop over.

3. **items()**: The items function is like a combination of **keys** and **values**. Instead of giving you one value at a time, it gives you a key and value pair for each entry in the dictionary. It is a little confusing, but all you need to know is that each element in the list consists of a key and the corresponding value. For the *pirate_dict*, the result would be this:

   pirate_dict.items() -> [("hello", "ahoy"), ("friend", "matey"), ("yes", "aye"), ("no", "nay")]

page = page+1 # 56

The resulting list has four key-value pairs that are very useful to loop over since it combines the keys and values of the dictionary.

4. **get()**: Before I talk about this last function, there is one question that you might be asking: what happens if you try to find a value for a key that doesn't exist in the dictionary? Well, the computer doesn't know what to do so it gives an error. The **get** function is an alternative way to access a value with a key where if the key is not in the dictionary, it returns **None** instead of erroring out.
   For our dictionary, you could use it like this:
   pirate_dict.get("hello") -> "ahoy"

   This would indeed do the same thing as the other method:
   pirate_dict["hello"] -> "ahoy"

   However, when you try using a key that isn't in the dictionary like "treasure":
   pirate_dict["treasure"] -> error

   This common method will error out while the get function will not:
   pirate_dict.get("treasure") -> None

   I know this might seem like it isn't a big deal, but trust me, we will be using this a lot later in the book.

Now that we know how to use a dictionary somewhat let's have a plan for the program:

1. Create English to Pirate dictionary
2. Get English sentence from the user
3. Loop through the dictionary and translate/substitute words
4. Print translation

Okay, now that we have a real plan, we can start creating the English to pirate dictionary. You probably haven't yet got into the hang of creating dictionaries, so look back at how I made the *pirate_dict*, and feel free to add many more words that can be translated.

Next, just as we have done in the previous two problems, ask and get an English sentence from the user to translate. If you're having trouble, you can either go back to the first part, where we talk about **input** or look at the previous programs we made together.

Alright, now we are on the meat of the project. We must try to loop through the dictionary and translate those words if they are in the sentence. When you look at this problem carefully, you'll probably notice that we've already talked about looping through dictionaries... and you're right! What dictionary function would be best to get both the English word and its pirate version?

You're right! We're going to use the **items()** function! (I have no idea if you got that right, but I'm just going to get on with it.)

Before coding, you might think about how to initialize the loop because each element in the list returned by **items()** has two values. So, normally, I would make you try to do it yourself, but honestly, this isn't an easy concept to understand, so here is the code for that:

```
for word, pirate_word in pirate_dict.items():
```

page = page+1 # 58

Instead of having one loop variable, we use two: word for the key (English word) and *pirate_word* for the value. We do this since each element of the items list contains two values, allowing us to split the pair into two variables. Again, just like other concepts, it is okay if you don't completely understand it, as we'll be using similar techniques for just about everything in this book.

Now that we have the loop down, all we have to do is check the sentence for words and replace them with *pirate_word*. To do this simply, we can use another Python library: **re**. Just like the **random** library, it has many functions, and feel free to look up what they all do, but I'm only going to go over the one we need now.

- **sub**: This function is a tool that finds specific values in strings and replaces them with other values. Suppose you wrote an essay for school about how cats make people lose sleep, but you accidentally wrote dog instead of cat everywhere! You could use this function like this:

```
essay = re.sub("dog", "cat", essay)
```

In this example, we're substituting dog for cat everywhere in the essay. Similarly, we can use it to replace numbers and many other patterns in a string.

I don't know about you, but after discovering the **sub** function, it seemed like it was made for this program! Anyway, I think you should try to figure out how you can use it, just like how I used it for the *essay* in our original program. Don't worry; if you don't know how to, you can check the solution at the end of the book, but PLEASE try and do it yourself first. Alright, enough of preaching; let's finish off this program.

The last step is to print the final translation; you can do this in any way you want (I would recommend using **f-strings** to be descriptive, but you do you).

Before finishing the program, look over it and test any edge cases. For example, I bet you haven't checked for capitalization cases. Did you ensure that if words in the input sentence are capitalized, they become lowercase before you substitute them? Otherwise, as I told you in the previous project, the program won't work because the computer treats uppercase and lowercase as different words.

After you've done all that, I think it's the end of yet another program! This is what? The third program, right? And you're already getting better at a much faster rate than me... you are destined to be a GOAT. Am I right, or am I right? Anyway, now your problems with trying to quote Jack Sparrow are over, and you are well on your way to becoming a fluent pirate!

Review:

- Dictionaries
  - Lists vs Dictionaries
  - Various dictionary methods
  - Looping through dictionary items
- Python module: re (regex or regular expression)

For GOATs: Create a dictionary with all your friends' names as keys, and random pirate characters in the movies as values. It's a fun game to see how your friends are linked to a pirate character.

Gen Alpha to Parent Translator (and vice versa)

First things first, isn't this almost the same thing as the last program? Yes, it is. But I really wanted to include this because it's just funny to see the differences between how the new generation speaks and the older generation. I mean. Have you ever been talking with your friends and your parents, who just don't understand what you're saying? It's hilarious, and because of that, I say we should add this program and get on with it!

Alright, this program is just a two-way translator between how this generation speaks and how parents speak and because it is very similar to the English to pirate program, it should be much easier to complete. There are some differences, the main one being that it is a two-way translator—meaning, we should code for a translation from Gen-Alpha to parent and vice versa. It is double the code, but now we can use it both ways!

Anyway, I know that the game plan for this program is almost the same as the pirate translator, but we should still make a plan because it is good practice and helps a lot when coding. So here it is...

1. Create a "Gen-Alpha to parent" dictionary
2. Ask whether the user is translating from Gen-Alpha to parent or from parent to Gen-Alpha
3. Get the sentence from the user
4. Loop through the dictionary and translate/substitute words
5. Print translation

As I said, the outline is very similar to our English to Pirate program, so you should already be able to do most of these things. Firstly, creating the dictionary should be no sweat because we've already made one for the previous problem. If you want, you can just take that dictionary and change the keys and values accordingly, where the keys are English words and their Gen-Alpha versions.

The next step is a bit different since we must ask the user if they translate a typical sentence to a Gen-Alpha sentence or vice versa. Usually, people do this by asking it straight up in the input prompt like so:

```
choice = input ("Enter 1 if translating from parent to Gen-Alpha,
               enter 2 if translating from Gen-Alpha to parent: ")
```

If we ask this in the input, all the user has to do in the input is type 1 or 2 based on what they want to do. This works well because then we can use a simple **if** condition to make the computer translate according to the user's choice. I won't show the specific condition for the **if** statement because I believe you can do it yourself. Remember, if you get stuck, you can always look back on previous problems and examples I gave in the book.

The next step is to get the sentence from the user. We can do this exactly how we did it in the pirate translator program. Of course, it'll be good to change the actual input prompt a bit to match this program, but it doesn't matter much as long as it is descriptive enough that the user would know what to do.

The fourth step is to loop through the dictionary and translate the words. We can do this by using the **items**() function in dictionaries to get both the keys and values. Also, using the **re** library, we can easily substitute words with their Gen-Alpha and normal versions depending on the type of translation. However, there is one difference between how we substitute for both types of translations.

If the user wants to translate a normal sentence into Gen-Alpha speak, we can use a similar code as the pirate translator:

```
sentence = re.sub(word, gen_alpha_word, sentence)
```

However, what do you think will happen if we use the same code to translate a Gen-Alpha sentence back into normal speech? Will it work just fine? If you said that it won't work, you are correct! The dictionary will still look for the normal word and replace it with the Gen-Alpha version. It won't do the vice versa that we want. There is a simple fix for this:

```
sentence = re.sub(gen_alpha_word, word, sentence)
```

All I did was switch the word and gen_alpha_word variables around. In this code, the computer will search for the Gen-Alpha word and replace it with the word rather than the other way around. A thing to note from this is that the order in which you put the variables in a function is <u>very</u> important, and you'll learn about this when we get to functions later.

Anyways, the final step is to print out the new, translated sentence. Now, either you can print the bare variable without any description... or you can use **f-strings** to print with a description like this:

```
print (f "Here is the translation: {sentence}")
```

Lastly, it is time for the edge cases! Before I tell you a type of edge case that could happen in this program, why don't you take some time to think?

Alright, I expect that you've taken some time, and by time, I mean 10 minutes. Not one, not two, and not five. 10 minutes. Okay, the edge case I wanted to add is what if some user inputs a number that isn't 1 or 2. The program won't break, but it won't print or output anything, leaving the user just guessing why it's taking so long or why it isn't doing anything. Fortunately, there is a simple fix... yup! Adding an **else** on the first user choice **if** condition with a print statement. You could really say anything as long as it tells the user how his input is incorrect, but I did something like this:

```
print ("You didn't choose 1 or 2")
```

It really can be as simple as that. As long as you are being as descriptive as possible so that the user understands your outputs, it doesn't matter. And that brings this translator to a close! I want to say that this translator went by much faster than the last one did, but that's partly because I believe that you guys can start working independently instead of me showing you how to do everything.

Review:

A fun game for extra practice of using:

- Dictionaries
- f-strings
- re module

For GOATs: Add multiple "slang modes" (TikTok, gamer, emoji). Let parents pick how wild the translation gets — from formal to full chaos.

Caesar Cipher

I don't know about you, but when I was younger, I was obsessed with these coded messages. Everyone is different, but I've felt like most people think that Morse code and other types of secure communication are just flat-out cool. And if that's the case for you, this is about to be an interesting and fun program!

Before beginning the code, there are many types of ciphers and methods to encode messages and whatnot, but the easiest way is with the Caesar cipher. But what is the Caesar cipher?

You probably already have done Caesar ciphers before and just didn't know the name. Basically, it is a type of encoding that just shifts all letters in a message by some number. For example, let's say we're shifting a message by three. This is how each letter would change:

- **A** becomes **D**
- **B** becomes **E**
- **C** becomes **F**
- …
- …
- **X** wraps around to become **A**
- **Y** wraps around to become **B**
- **Z** wraps around to become **C**

If you want more practice, take these sentences here and try to shift it by three:

- **I am fat** becomes **L dp idw**
- **I like pineapples on pizza** becomes **L olnh slqhdssohv rq slccd**
- **Why am I here?** Becomes **Zkb dp L khuh?**

Now that you know what a Caesar cipher is and how to do it, we can figure out how to do it in code. With our current information in coding, we don't know how to do this. But that's what all the built-in functions are for! Before learning about them, I think it's time to tell you about Unicode values.

Computers don't understand letters; For example, when you type the letter A, the computer assigns a number and stores A as 65. These numbers are standardized and called Unicode, where every character has a unique Unicode value. In this system, uppercase "A" has a Unicode value 65, and the uppercase "B" has 66. Similarly, the lowercase "a" has a Unicode value of 97, and the lowercase "b" has 98. Something to remember is that the distance between the letters remains the same in Unicode system as well. For example, A and C are separated by one letter. This chart should give you an idea about that:

https://www.cs.cmu.edu/~pattis/15-1XX/common/handouts/ascii.html

We can take two main actions in Python with these Unicode values: meet **ord** and **chr**.

1. **ord**: This function gives the Unicode number for any character. For example, if we did something like this: **ord**("A"), it would return 65.

2. **chr**: This function does the exact opposite thing as **ord**. It takes a Unicode value and outputs the character. For example, **chr**(65) would return "A".

Using these two functions, we must create a formula that uses a character and some shift number as input and outputs the correct, shifted character. Anyway, while you're thinking about that, let's look at our program outline.

1. Get a message and shift the number
2. Loop through the message and shift every letter
3. Print encoded message

The first step in this process is very simple since we've done inputs since our first program. We'll need two inputs for this program, one for the actual message and one for shifting.

The next step is the bulk of the program. We have to loop through the entire message, going character by character. If you forgot how to do this, you could look back to the last part where we talked about loops, but it shouldn't be that hard because it is done in the same format as looping through a list.

After initializing the loop, we get to the hard part, where we must use our brains to develop a formula.

1. The first thing we have to do is get the Unicode value for the letter so we can start with:

   ```
   unicode_value = ord(letter)
   ```

2. Next, find the character's position in the 26-letter English Alphabet. So, we should subtract 65 since that's when the Unicode values for letters start at (lowercase "a"). To do this:

   ```
   letter_position = ord(letter) - 65
   ```

3. Find the letter's position after shifting. So, add the shift number, which gives us the following:

   ```
   new_letter_position = ord(letter) + shift - 65
   ```

4. But what if the shifting makes the letter go beyond 26? We'll have to use the mod operator %. If you don't know, the mod operator just gives us the remainder after dividing a number by another. This gives us:

page = page+1 # 70

```
new_letter_position  = new_letter_position % 26
```

5. Now we have our new letter position from 1 to 26, but to make it a Unicode value, we have to add back 65 to it, giving us the following:

```
new_unicode_value = new_letter_position + 65
```

6. Finally, we can use the chr function to make the value into an actual letter like this:

```
new_letter = chr(new_unicode_value)
chr((ord(letter) + shift - 65) % 26 + 65)
```

One cool way to write all the above steps is to do this:

```
new_letter = chr((ord(letter) + shift - 65) % 26 + 65)
```

That's not all, though, because it is different with lowercase letters. After all, they start at a Unicode value of 97 with lowercase a. In that case, all we have to do is replace the 65 with 97. This gives us two similar formulas for both lowercase and uppercase letters, which means that we need to have conditions checking whether each letter in the message is uppercase or lowercase.

Fortunately, look no further, as more built-in functions are coming to the rescue!

1. **Islower()**: This function gets a string and checks if every letter in the string is lowercase. Essentially, it is just a condition; if matched, it will output True. On the other hand, if even one character is uppercase, it will return False.

2. **Isupper()**: This function is much like **islower()**, and it's the same thing but with uppercase strings. Also, you can use it in ways exactly like **islower,** with the same syntax, use cases, and all!

We can make conditional statements now that we have specific functions acting as conditions for our letters. Because this is a bit new, I'll give you the code you need to run for each letter in the sentence. Yes! Loop through the input sentence, just like how you loop through a list. Don't forget to initialize the variable *encoded_message* to an empty string before the **for** loop.

```
if letter.isupper() == True:
    encoded_message += chr((ord(letter) + shift - 65) % 26 + 65)
elif letter.islower() == True:
    encoded_message += chr((ord(letter) + shift - 97) % 26 + 97)
```

Take a good look at this code and test it out yourself. One thing you might be wondering about is the +=. This does work even though you can't technically add strings since Python treats it as just adding a letter to the end of the string, which is *encoded_message*. The final part of this program is to print the encoded message, and a simple print statement will work (maybe you can use **f-strings** to be more descriptive).

Wait, wait, wait... it's time for everyone's favorite part of the program: the edge cases! Just like usual, I have an edge case for this program. However, after this program, I want you to go out of your way to find and fix edge cases without waiting for me to tell you. This would be good practice; even professional coders sometimes have trouble with this, so it's never too early to start. Well, without further ado, the edge case for this program is what if a letter in the sentence is not uppercase or lowercase; in fact, it isn't a letter at all but some other symbol.

You might think the **islower** and **isupper** functions will somehow handle this, but nope. You also might be thinking that in the Caesar cipher, symbols like the question mark or the semi-colon are just left out, but that also doesn't happen. To leave the symbols as is, all you have to do is add an **else** statement at the end of the conditions like this:

```
else:
    encoded_message += letter
```

And voila! After you add this little snippet of code, you are finally finished with your very own message encoder! Now you don't have to worry about anybody reading your diary or texts! Bye-bye, snoopy parents, they'll never be able to figure it out. Wait… what if you can't solve your own encoded messages anymore? You need to find a way to decode your messages, too, right? I'll leave that up to you, but I hint that to build a decoder, you don't have to do much coding at all.

One thing though, before moving on: if you find a way to build a decoder, ensure you don't give it to anyone… Otherwise, they could read your messages just like before, and all your hard work would go to waste!

Review:

- Introduction to Unicode values
- Conversion from Alphabet to Unicode
- Functions: ord and chr
- String functions: islower, isupper

 **For GOATs**: Create an extended version of a cipher using a custom key. Use the Unicode of your key to shift each letter in the message. For example, if your key is "GOAT", apply its Unicode (71, 79, 65, 84) repeatedly across the entire message to encrypt it. This method makes decryption significantly more challenging.

Guess the Number

Have you ever played the Guess the Number game? If you're anything like me, you probably haven't heard of this game until now, and honestly, that's probably a good thing. I'm not saying this is a bad game, but it'll get quite boring for anybody over nine after a couple of rounds.

The game goes like this: first, player one picks a random number from 1 to 100, then player two tries to guess the number. The twist is, every time player-two guesses, player-one gives them a hint: whether the number is higher or lower than, or equal to, the guessed number! The final thing to note is that player two gets seven guesses to get the number.

Before jumping into this problem, I want you to look at this game and try to devise a strategy if you are player-two. How would you use higher or lower information to develop an accurate plan? If your plan is anything like what I will show you, you are doing great! If it is completely different, you are still doing great!

The main strategy when coding this problem, and if you are player-two in the game, is to use the **binary search** method. Now, what is binary search? Binary search is a method where, given some range, your guess should always be at the midpoint. This way, you are cutting the range in half, no matter if the actual number is higher or lower.

For example, let's say the random number is 78, and we guess 50. player-one will tell us that the number is higher, eliminating every number from 1 to 50. Our next guess will be the midpoint of our new range: 50 to 100, which is 75. In this way, we can keep guessing until we get the number. Now, let's say we tried guessing something like 25. player-one would, again, tell us that the actual number is higher, but this time, it would only eliminate 25 numbers, putting us in a much worse spot. Looking at this now, you might think we should guess 75 or something close to it. However, the problem is that if you always guess 75, there is more of a chance for the number to be lower, which puts us in a worse spot again.

Binary Search

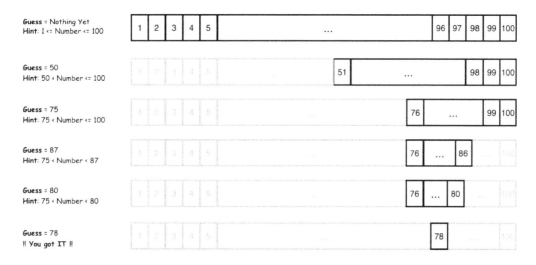

After learning about the binary search algorithm, you might think about how a simple thing like this can be important in the real world. The reality is that though it's simple, it's used effectively in technology around the world in various complex ways, like searching for a word in the dictionary or finding a contact in the phone book.

We can get into the main coding part now that you know binary search. And you know what that means... outline time!

1. Select a random number

2. Make game variables

3. Repeatedly ask for guesses and tell the user higher or lower

4. Check if they won or not

Remember when we were introduced to the **random** library for this first step. What were the functions that we talked about? Which one of those functions should we use? Once you figure that out, I would probably set the range from 1 to 100, but that's entirely up to you. One thing to note is that if you want the range to be smaller or bigger, make sure to give them fewer or more chances accordingly.

Now, let's look at step two. What variables do you think we should use in this program? Since it is the first time you need a good number of variables, I'll give them to you, but keep in mind that we're entering the big leagues… most programs from here on out will use variables regularly. Also, for future programs, I'm not talking about this step as much because, as I said, this is the big leagues!

For this program, these are the variables that I used in my code (obviously, you can change the names to whatever you like, but make sure to keep them simple):

- *secret_number -> the random number that the user will try to guess*
- *guesses_taken -> the amount of guesses the user has taken (starts at zero)*
- *max_guesses -> the maximum amount of guesses the user can take (make it 7)*

With the variables out of the way, let's look at the main part of the game: the loop. A thing to consider when coding this loop is that though we have a maximum number of guesses, we don't know how long this loop will take because it depends on the user's guessing ability. Knowing this, consider the differences between **for** and **while** loops and consider which type of loop we should use.

That's right! We should use the while loop because we don't know exactly how many times to loop. However, we can't use the **while** loop just like that; we need to find a condition that makes the loop go. To find this, let's first consider the opposite: *a condition ending the* *game.* The game ends when either the user runs out of guesses or the user correctly guesses the number. To reverse this condition back, all you have to do is logically think about it, and we get something like this:

```
while guess != secret_number and guesses_taken < max_guesses:
```

But not so fast… there's one problem with this condition. We don't have the guess variable yet because we haven't asked for the user's guess. If you remember our first problem together (talking about even before the magic 8 ball), we had a similar problem. This is because the **scope** of the guess variable is not large enough since we will be creating the variable <u>inside</u> the while loop. For this reason, we cannot use the first part of the condition, and the while loop will look like this:

```
while guesses_taken < max_guesses:
```

However, because that is a big part of the game's ending, we will have to code that inside the loop, probably using a **break** statement, just like we did in that program in the introduction anyhow, which leads up to the first thing we have to do in the loop, which is getting the guess from the user. Since we've done this many times, I think I will let you do that part by yourself… yes, I am. Along with that, we also have to increase *guesses_taken* by one (I don't think I have to explain that; it's pretty straightforward).

Now it's time to code the higher or lower feedback to the guess! And what better to use than a simple **if** condition? This should be pretty straightforward, but I'll start it right here:

```
if guess < secret_number
    print ("Too low!")
```

You can also use the same format if the guess is too high. Also, here is the perfect place to add the condition if the user has guessed it right. Don't forget to print an output message (use **f-strings** to include how many guesses they took) and have a **break** statement to get out of the loop and end the game.

Now that the loop is finished, it's time to print a failure message for the people who did not get the right answer. However, you can't just print out the message because we don't know if the user has won. For example, if the user got it right and the computer broke out of the loop, it would print out the failure message! To fix this, we can use another **if** condition just checking if the reason why the game ended was that the user ran out of guesses just like this:

```
if guesses_taken > max_guesses:
```

Again, don't forget to write that failure output message, including the number. Before we move on, try playing this game and using the binary search method to beat the computer. I guarantee that using that method will beat the computer at least 100 percent of the time! Wait. I can guarantee you beat it 100 percent when the range is from 1 to 100, and you get 7 chances.

And from my understanding, I think you're done with this program! Not only that, but that concludes this first beginner part of this book! To whoever made it this far without passing out from cringy jokes or unfunny programs, bravo! You are about ⅓ of the way from becoming a cool coder!

Review:

In this section, we used an interesting and powerful technique to show how searching for an element in a sorted list could be so much faster:

- Binary search

- Linear search vs binary search

 **For GOATs:** Find an integer in a sorted list. Show the difference between linear search and binary search by finding the time it takes for the computer to find a number in a randomly generated list of numbers. See how the time increases with increase in the size of the list.

Part 2: Middle Grounds

010: NOVICE

Alright rookie, you've probably got the basics down now. Just to make sure though, you should know print statements, loops, conditions, among many more topics, to enter this part. You see, coders don't just write smaller snippets; we craft experiences. So in Part 2, we will leave the training wheels behind and dive into projects that'll make you feel like a novice.

Here, you'll take everything you learned about variables, dictionaries, etc., and level them up. We're talking about full-blown games like Hangman, where you'll start to track guesses and learn the art of displaying text. You'll build a working Tic Tac Toe, where you can play anyone at anytime. And just when you think you've got it figured out, we'll throw in everyone's favorite: War (a.k.a. the longest card game ever).

But the most important thing you should take from this is: functions. This piece of code is going to be your best friend for a long time in the coding world. Now, I will get into what they are much more in depth, but here's what you should know about them: think of functions like your favorite fast-food combo. You don't need to know how the kitchen makes those fries and burgers, you just say "Combo #3", and you get your food. Functions work the same way: write the recipe once, and you can use it forever. Trust me, once you start thinking in functions (which I'll teach you in this part), you'll never code the same way again.

Hangman

Hangman is one of those games where you could hop in a time travel machine, go a hundred years in the future, and there will still be kids playing it with their friends. You can't tell me you haven't enjoyed playing this game because I believe that isn't true. However, I also know there probably have been times when you've wanted to play Hangman, but everyone else is busy…and that's where this program comes in!

For this program, we basically just want the computer to act like another player, specifically the player who already knows the word. Unlike what we did in the previous part, I want you to create an outline for this program. Wait, wait, wait. First, let me talk to you about one of the most important things in coding for any language: **functions**.

Okay, I know that we've talked a little about it, like the functions for dictionaries, strings, and functions we use from Python libraries. But now I'm going to go more in-depth and teach you how to create your own!

Consider a school setting where a 9-hour school day is divided into, let's say, 7 periods, each period for a different subject. Imagine a school with the same 9-hour school day allotted to learn one subject - Algebra for nine hours straight? I would pass out!

Anyways, you might be thinking about what I'm trying to explain here. Just think about school as this 9-hour long task. This task is divided into classes which act as subtasks. Even further, each class is broken down into multiple slots for different assignments, projects, discussions, and activities. Believe it or not, it's done this way because it's the most effective for students and teachers. And it's the exact same thing with coding.

Let's say that someone is doing a massive coding project, and they are doing it as one enormous task. The problem with this is that it will become hard to read and understand, and at some point, even the person will have trouble navigating it. Not to mention that coding projects can get unmotivating if they are done as one large blob rather than being divided into tiny parts. That is where functions come in. They're used as subtasks in a coding project, making it easier to read, test out, navigate, and look better. You might think that it's just words and numbers, but the reality is that looking neat and nice is an underrated part of coding.

First things first, let's look at the syntax of a function:

```
def function_name(parameters):
    # some code
    return value
```

Before we go further like looking at examples, let's take a look at all the components of starting a function that are in the above snippet:

- **def** -> The keyword that tells the computer that the following lines are part of a function
- **function_name** -> This is where you write your descriptive function name
- **parameters** -> These are optional inputs that you can pass to the function. This is because any variable outside the function cannot be used inside the function. In other words, the outside variables don't have the **scope** (unless declared **global**). This is the same with the variables made and changed inside the function
- **return** -> This is how the function outputs, though it is also optional. Because variables that are changed in the function aren't changed outside of the function (except for specific data types, which will be discussed later). In most cases, we return something out.

Now, let's look at an example function that adds two numbers:

```
def add(a, b):
    result = a + b
    return result
```

In this function, the name of it is *add,* and the parameters (inputs) we give are the variables *a* and *b*. Inside the function, it just adds them up, puts the total in the *result* variable, and returns it. The next thing to look at with functions is how to actually call (use) them. For the function above, here is what we would do if we wanted to add 7 + 3:

```
sum_of_numbers = add (7, 3)
```

To call a function, you have to code it in this format: function_name(parameter1, parameter2). This is important because the number of parameters and their types that you make when defining the function need to be the same when calling the function. Again, there are exceptions. Otherwise, the program will break and error out.

Also, to call a function, you don't need to make a variable, but because we are returning the result of the function, we should store it in the *sum_of_numbers* variable. Printing *sum_of_numbers* would give us the sum, which is 10. Why don't you try this out and, while you're at it, create and call some functions of your own?

Now, I'm not sure if you caught this or not, but when you see how a function can get called and how its parameters can affect what it returns, there is another clear advantage. It's reusable. Since a function can be called multiple times with an availability to change, it can be used to replace code that is repeated throughout a project. This makes the code itself smaller and can help people avoid writing the same stuff over and over again. Now, there are other advantages of functions, so feel free to explore and find out what those are out in your own time, because it truly is fantastic!

One more thing to mention with functions is that, honestly, putting any code into a function is just good practice and will help make your code neat and clear. Before actually starting this hangman game, try putting all your previous programs into one big function and try calling it. It should do the exact same thing, and because you don't need to give any inputs, parameters aren't required.

Alrighty, I think that covers functions, and that takes us straight into our Hangman game. Honestly, I know that it's just been like two lines since I talked about functions, but I think we should just start using them in this program, and because of that, I'll come up with the gameplan for this project:

1. Choose a random word
2. Make game variables
3. Game loop
   a. Display status of word
   b. Get guess
   c. Check if guess is in word
   d. Add guess to guessed letters
   e. Check if all letters in word have been guessed
4. Print win or lose statement

When I look at this outline, I see places where we can divide the immense task of the hangman game into subtasks for functions. Firstly, let's make *choosing a random word* into a function. I know that you guys can code it just fine, but why not make it a challenge by making you write your own function?

Let's look at this. The function should return a randomly selected word, but it doesn't need any parameters because we can just have a word list within it. Knowing all of this, we can make something like:

```python
def choose_word():
    word_list = ["python," "random," "hangman"]
    return random.choice(word_list)
```

First off, I want to say that in the *word_list*, you can put whatever and however many words you like. Second, isn't this much easier than you thought? I mean, all you are really doing is just adding a **def** statement and then returning the selected word. Everything else is what you have done and know already. Alright, do you understand it? Great!

Next, let's create a main function for the code that actually calls all the sub-functions. You can name the function anything you like, and because it's the main function that starts and ends it, there won't be any parameters. In this function, we first call the *choose_word* function and store it in some variable. Then, we can create the game variables like *guessed_letters* to store the letters already guessed and attempts to store how many attempts they have. If you need or think of any other variables, feel free to create them.

The next thing we can do is create the loop, and by looking back at our past programs and just your knowledge of **for** and **while** loops, you can figure out which type we will use right now. On top of that, try coming up with the condition for the loop as well since we have talked about that multiple times already.

Now that we are inside the loop, let's print the word. Actually, just make a function that prints the word; *display_word*. To actually print the word, we need to go over the word in a loop, and for every letter that has been guessed (using *guessed_letters*), we add the letter, and if it hasn't, we add an underscore to show a blank. Here is the snippet to do this:

```python
display = ""
for letter in word:
    if letter in guessed_letters:
        display += letter
    else:
        display += "_"
```

Also, using this code, you can probably figure out what parameters we would need in this function as well as what we should return back to the main function. (I don't know. It's probably the display, right?) Going back to the main function **while** loop, we should obviously print the displayed word using the function, giving it the required parameters.

The next thing to do is to get the guess from the user. I think this needs… you guessed it! Another function! In this function, all we need to do is ask the user for a letter to guess. However, if the letter is in the *guessed_letters* list, then we should ask for a new letter. Also, when we get the input from the user, make sure that it is lowercase so that the computer doesn't think the same letter is different because of their case.

For this function, we do need a loop, and you probably already know what parameter we need as well. Since you know most of the things to do in this function, I'll leave this up to you as well. Good luck! By the way, if you are struggling (honestly, I've been a bit lazy today, so you probably are), feel free to check the solutions at the link given at the end of the book.

Now that we've made the function, all we have to do is call it in the main function. Isn't this much easier than having to code everything in the same loop? Anyways, next up on our agenda is to check if the *guess* is actually in the word. And this is something you surely know: **if** conditions! Just to make sure though, if the *guess* is in the word, print a happy message, but if it isn't in the word, the attempts should get subtracted by one and the program should print a sad message…

Also, don't forget to add the *guess* to the *guessed_letters* list.

The final thing in this while loop (wow this is one huge program) is to check if the user has guessed all the letters. Doing this is a bit trickier than what we have done in the past, so I'll show you my code here:

```
if display_word(word, guessed_letters) == word:
    print (f" Congratulations! You've guessed the word {word}
correctly!")
    break
```

Basically, I'm using the *display_word* function, which returns the user-guessed word, and if the user has guessed all the words, it should return the same thing as the actual word. And if they are equal, then I'm printing a happy message and breaking out of this loop. But of course, if they aren't equal, then the loop must go on.

Now, after and outside the loop, we have to check if the loop just ended because the user ran out of attempts, and if that is the case, we should print a failure message, or if the loop just broke out because the user succeeded. To do this, a simple **if** condition checking if *attempts_left* is at zero will work, with a failure message being printed if it is.

Before we say sayonara to this hangman program, **do not forget to call the main function.** Seriously, if you don't call the main function that has the entire **while** loop and everything else, the code won't actually do anything, so that is extremely important.

Anyways, I kind of sped through this program; at least it went much faster than previously in part one, and this will be the case throughout the entire book because you have gotten much better, and frankly, you don't need me to be super descriptive about everything. But... since this is your first program without me really going in-depth about everything, why don't you take a look at the solution for this program at the end of the book? Even if you think you've understood it all, just take a look. And don't worry, I have comments on most lines explaining it all again (though briefly).

With that out of the way, I think some celebrating is needed! I mean, celebration is not for hanging a man – come to think of it, it's a dark name for a kid's game! Alright, you have just finished your first program with functions, and that needs some reward. Go ask your parents for a new video game or something because you definitely deserve it (whether your parents think so or not)!

Review:

Functions! Functions! Functions!
- Why functions?
- Syntax and structure of functions in Python
- Writing conditions on function output

For GOATs: Extend the program, get all the words from the English dictionary, and assign positive/negative scores with each correct and incorrect guess. If you are in the zone, you can also filter the words based on users' choice (ex: Movies, Music)

Matching Tiles

When you were younger, you might've heard your grandma cursing under her breath as she played some game on her phone. You probably didn't care and resumed playing by yourself. Well, that game your granny was playing is Memory, a.k.a Matching Tiles. Now, if that scenario somehow rings a bell, you don't know what this game is, though it is pretty straightforward. If you do know this game, well, still read this because I might play it differently than you do.

The game starts off with a board with all tiles facing down. Each tile has a number underneath it, and on each turn, the player must flip over precisely two of them. Each number on the board has a pair, and if the player flips over a pair, those tiles stay facing upwards and are revealed. The game ends when the player flips over all pairs, and all tiles are faced up.

Now, this seems like a big jump from the Hangman program, but like anything else we have done, splitting up this program into more manageable parts can make it much easier. Lucky for you, I have done just that with this game plan!

1. Create the game board
   a. Create random pairs of tiles
   b. Shuffle numbers and put them in a grid
2. Make game variables
3. Game Loop -- repeat until all tiles are revealed
   a. Display game board
   b. Get first tile from user and check if already revealed
   c. Get second tile from user and check if already revealed
   d. Check if tiles match
   e. Reveal or don't reveal tiles
4. Print number of moves

Alright, I think there's nothing better to do than just jump into it! Looking at the first step, we need to create the game board, which is a grid of tiles. But wait... how do you make a grid in Python? We know how to make a list, so would using that work? I'll give you some time to think about it before I give you some possible solutions. (Remember, it's essential that you try to challenge yourself on these questions; otherwise, you won't be learning.)

To properly make a grid of some sort in Python, we have to use a 2D array, which is basically an array inside of an array... cool, right? Anyways, to properly explain this, I need you to think of a 2D array as a classroom's desk arrangement. I don't know how your desks are placed, but for me, the desks were in a grid-like pattern: rows and columns, with one person sitting at one desk.

Now, there are two main ways to create a 2D array in Python. Both ways build off the concept that 2D arrays are, to put it simply, lists inside of lists.

1. **Method 1: Hardcoding Data**

```
twod_array = [
    [1, 2, 3],
    [4, 5, 6],
    [7, 8, 9]
]
```

Now you can see that whenever I was saying a 2d array is just a list inside of a list, you know, I wasn't joking. It really is this simple, and the syntax is just like a regular, one-dimensional Python list. Now, most of the time, 2d arrays are not created in this manner, where the values are already known and are **hardcoded** into the array at the initialization.

2. **Method 2: Using a Loop**

Now, if you don't want to hardcode (which is most of the time), you can also use a loop to create a 2D array. However, to do this, you must use what is called a nested for loop. Like a 2D array, a nested for loop is *a for loop inside a for loop.*

Think of a nested for loop like a clock. The outer loop (the small hand) moves once every time the inner loop (the big hand) completes a full cycle. Here, look at this code snippet and think of the output on your own. Then, try the snippet out in PyCharm and check if the result matches what you expected.

```python
for row in range(3):
    for col in range(3):
        print (f"{row}, {col} ")
```

As you can see, the syntax is very similar; in fact, it is the same as a normal **for** loop. Anyways, using this, how can we make a 2D array? And the bigger question is, how can we index a 2D array? Well, to find first element in first row of a 2D array: we do list[0][0] instead of list[0]

Which basically asks for the 2D array for the first list and then the first element of that first list. You can also think of it like coordinates on a graph, where the first index is the row, and the second index is the column the element is in. Now, to create a 2D array using a nested for loop, we can do something like this:

```python
grid = []
for row in range(3):
    line = []
    for col in range(3):
        line.append(0)
    grid.append(line)
```

Feel free to try this code snippet on your own, but this code just initializes and creates a 3x3 2D array that is filled with all zeros. And if you understand that, I think we are free to move on to the Matching Tiles program!

Now, before we can actually create the game board, we have to first randomly create the pairs of *tiles; we* have to shuffle them around. We've done this many times before using the **random.shuffle**() function. Oh, wait! That brings to my attention, for this program and all programs in the future, most of these steps should be made in and with their own function. So, for example, to create a function for this creating board process, I am doing this:

```
def generate_board():
```

But of course, feel free to change the function name to your liking. Anyways, you already know how to shuffle the list, and with all the knowledge you currently have, you should be able to create the *tiles* list and put random numbers using the **random.randint**() function as well, but if you are stuck, you can look at the solutions using the link given at the end of the book.

After creating the *tiles* list, now comes the hard part of actually transforming that 1D array into the 2D array. Since this is your first time using 2D arrays and all, I will give you the code to do this:

```
board = []
tiles_idx = 0
for i in range(4):
    board.append([])
    for j in range(4):
        board.append(tiles[tiles_idx])
        tiles_idx += 1
```

At first glance, this code looks very complicated, but in reality, it's not. To transform that 1D array (*tiles*) into a 2D array (*board*), you need to use a separate index that isn't given by the **for** loop to keep track of what index the iteration is currently on for the *tiles* list. The *tiles* list is a 1D array, so its index won't be [0][0], [0][1], etc.; it will be [0], [1], [2], etc. The last thing to do in this step is to just return the board.

The next step in this process is to make the game variables. Now, before I tell you anything, what game variables do you think we will need? That's right! First, we need the *board*, which we can just use the function that we made in the last step. We also need a separate 2D array to keep track of what tiles are revealed and what tiles are not revealed. To do this, we just have to create another 2D array and fill it with the Boolean value of **False**. This way, if a certain element in the revealed grid is False, it has not been correctly matched and revealed. If it's True, it has been correctly matched and therefore, revealed. Finally, we also need a variable to keep track of how many moves or turns the player has used.

Now that we have the game variables, it's finally time to start the game loop. The first thing we do when creating any loop is to figure out whether we should use a **for** loop or a **while** loop. In this case, we don't know exactly how many moves or iterations the user will need, so this means we will use a... **while** loop! We will loop until the player has correctly matched and revealed every tile. But how do we check that? Well, that's where the revealed grid comes in! And in fact, we should make, you guessed it, another function! For this function, all we have to do is check if all elements in the revealed 2D array is True, and if they are, we return True; if they aren't, we return False. To do this, we have to loop through the 2D array and use an **if** condition to check each element's value. This could be a bit challenging yet a simple task, so I'll leave you to it.

To actually use this function in the **while** loop, the loop's initialization should look like this:

```
while not is_complete(revealed):
```

Now, keep in mind, *is_complete* is the function that we just created to check if all the tiles are matched and revealed. Anyways, getting on to the next step, we have to display the game board. What better way to do this than by using another function? Yeah, I know this might be getting boring, always using a function and all, but seriously, functions are the real building blocks of great coding.

Technically, you can display the 2D grid of the matching tiles however you want, but for simplicity, I wanted to have unrevealed tiles as a * and revealed tiles as whatever their number was. So, you can do whatever you want in this function as long as you print out a 2D array (remember, you have to use a nested for loop).

The next couple of steps are things that you (hopefully!) know how to do it. We need to ask and get the player's choice for their first tile to flip. To do this, we can ask for the "x" and "y" coordinates of the tile they want to reveal on the board. Next, if that tile is already revealed, we need them to pick again. However, if all goes well, we need to get their choice for the second tile to flip and, again, make sure that it isn't already revealed. Finally, we have to check if both tiles match and keep them revealed if they do. If they don't match, "unreveal" both the tiles (flip them back down), and a new iteration starts.

Oh, wait! I almost forgot to mention this, but don't forget to increment the *moves* variable to keep track of how many turns they take because once they match all the tiles, we must

page = page+1 # 100

print out how many turns they took to finish. This leads to the last step of this program, which is actually outside of the game loop, but it is the winning statement. Because this game doesn't have a winner and loser (it goes until the entire board is finished, no matter what), the statement is a generic one. We've been doing these win-or-lose statements for a while now, so I'll give you a chance to come up with your own. Remember to include how many moves they took.

Wow! It looks like we are finished with this program! I'd say that this was the biggest program that you've done by a mile, and you took it with no sweat. I will say, from now on, the programs will get bigger, harder, and gnarlier (is that a word people say nowadays?), but I have utmost faith in you.

Also, just like this program, a lot of the minor sub-tasks that you have done in some way, shape, or form, I will make you do them yourself from now on because otherwise, this book would be a thousand pages long, and I don't want to be sitting on a desk writing all that. However, I will still teach you all the things that you don't know in-depth, so there is that. However, don't expect as many hints on things you should be able to know. Worst comes to worst, you can look at your past programs to see how to do these things. Well, if all is well, I think it's time to take a small break and then move on to the next program!

Wait, wait, before you move on to the next program... don't forget to call the main function! I almost forgot as well, but you need to do that. Also, you can check my solutions if you are stuck on any part.

Review:
- Plan and divide your complex programs into sub-tasks

- Introduction to 2-dimensional lists

    o How to create

    o Access elements at desired position

- Looping through 2D lists

- Using more functions from random module

For GOATs: Extend this program by nXn tile sizes, add score for each right/wrong choices, add more themes (animals, movies), add a timer.

Tic Tac Toe

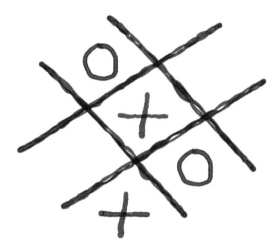

Alright, let's rewind to the dark ages—you know before you had phones, computers, or anything cool. Yeah, back when you were in school on a rainy day, stuck in the classroom during recess with nothing but paper, pencils, and your imagination.

So, what was THE game everyone played when they were bored in class? If you just thought, "**Pac-Man!**"—Nah, that needs a screen. **Chess?** Too complicated.

But if you guessed **Tic Tac Toe**, congrats! You win... absolutely nothing. But hey, it's the right answer! Today, I'm going to show you how to code Tic Tac Toe. Buckle up—it's going to be way more fun than that time you kept drawing X's and O's until your notebook turned into a chaotic mess.

I'm not going to explain a game that literally fits on a sticky note. But hey, if you somehow missed out on playing it, just Google it or check Wikipedia.

Now, in this program, we're coding Tic Tac Toe so that two actual humans can play against each other. No AI, no computer opponent—just you and a friend, face to face, battling for bragging rights. And yeah, I know most games end in a draw because, let's be honest, the strategy isn't rocket science. But if that happens, just settle it the old-fashioned way—rock-paper-scissors, arm wrestling, or just straight-up declaring yourself the winner.

Anyways, let's move on to the game plan for this program:

1. Create the (for now empty) board
2. Create game variables
3. Game Loop
    a. Display the board
    b. Get either player-one or player-two move
    c. Check if move is valid
    d. Update the board (X or O)
    e. Check if game is over

This is very similar to the previous two game programs in this chapter, and at this point, I think you notice a trend in this chapter of the book: games. Yes, this chapter is about games, and because of that, the game variables, game loop, and win/lose statements are all going to be involved in some way in all these programs, so you will see similarities between all the programs. But honestly, that's better for you because you will be able to really master these techniques!

Getting into it, to create the game board, we already know, based on the Matching Tiles program, that we need to create a 2D array. Fortunately, we also already talked about how to create a 2D array using a nested **for** loop! That should give you a clear idea of how to make a function that creates this game board. Make sure you create the 2D array *board* with "-" though (Wow, that step was simple enough!)

```python
board = []
for row in range(3):
    line = []
    for col in range(3):
        line.append("-")
```

The next step in this program is creating the game variables. For this step, I'll again let you think about what variables we will need... yeah, you thought I was going to give you the answers just like that, right? Nope. In fact, I'm not going to say the variables here. You've been creating game variables for quite a bit now, so you should get the hang of it. Of course, I'm not going to leave you all in the dark, though. You can still look at my solutions, but again, like I've said many, many times before, don't look at them without spending time trying them yourself.

Don't forget that throughout all of this, it is important to add print statements that describe the program. For example, before the game variables and game loop, you could add something like this to give a better experience for the user:

```python
print ("Welcome to Tic Tac Toe!")
```

Now, let's move on to the main portion of any game program: the game loop. First things first, what type of loop should we use in this game: **for** loop or **while** loop? Well, we don't know exactly how many turns the game will take, but we do know some conditions...

page = page+1 # 105

which means we should use a **while** loop. However, we actually have multiple ways the game could end. Unlike the last program, matching tiles, the game could end with a definite winner or a draw where the entire board is filled out, but there is no winner. Because of this, we will need to add these conditions inside of the **while** loop. This means the initialization of the **while** loop will just be this:

```
while True:
```

The next step inside of the game loop is to format and display the current board, whether it's empty or filled with some Xs and Os. And for this, what better to use than another function! For this, you can format it however you want, or you can also just look at some of my past formats or some of your past formats. Honestly, this isn't a big deal since it's not really a Python concept or idea; it's just styling, so here is how I did it:

```
for row in board:
    print (" | ".join(row))
    print ("-" * 10)
```

At first look at this snippet, you're probably wondering what in the world **join()** is. And to anybody who doesn't know a certain Python keyword, that's the exact response they would have as well. The **join()** function just combines elements from a list (which, in this case, is row in the board) into a string, using a character as a separator between each list element. So, for example, the list ["X," "O", "X"] would become "X|O|X". The next line is also most likely new to you, but it's really nothing hard. It just prints the character "-" five times. That asterisk acts literally like a multiplier and just multiplies it five times. When some cells are placed with Xs and Os, board will display as shown:

```
-  |  0  |  0
------------
-  |  X  |  -
------------
X  |  X  |  0
------------
```

Now for this display function, does the function have to return anything? I'll let you think of the answer for that yourself, but now, we have to move on to the next step.

The next step in this game loop is getting the player's move. In this, however, there is another step: we first have to figure out whose turn it is. This seems very simple to us, but to the computer, it's not so simple. To solve this problem in a computer-esque way, we have to first think like a computer. Let's take an example.

- Turn 1 -> Player 1
- Turn 2 -> Player 2
- Turn 3 -> Player 1
- Turn 4 -> Player 2
- Turn 5 -> Player 1
- Etc.

Looking at this, try to see if there are any patterns. I don't know about you, but there seems to be a pretty clear pattern. If the turn number is odd, it's always the player one's turn. If the turn number is even, it's always player-two's turn. Now, using the mod (%) operator that we talked about way back in chapter one, and a proper game variable to keep track of what turn it is (now do you understand why game variables are very important!), we can easily figure this out. A simple **if** condition can tell the computer whose turn it is, and once we know that, we can then ask for what move the user wants to play. To do this, we can ask for the "x" and "y" coordinates of the cell they want to place on the board.

Now that we have that information, the next step is to validate the user's input. Before I just give away all the answers like I'm Santa, why don't you take some time to think about what constraints we should put in place to validate the input? Yes! I'm hoping you got that right... But anyways, we need to make sure that both inputs are less than 3 and that the actual board space is empty. Why less than three if the grid is a 3x3, you might ask? (There's no way you actually asked that, but just play along.) Well, Python starts with the index of zero, so you might want to specify that in the **input()** prompt so that the player knows to put whatever coordinates they thought but minus one.

After all has been validated, we then have to update the board using indexing like this:

```
board[row][col] = current_player
```

Note that *current_player* is just X or O. Anyways, after updating, we have to check if there is a winner, and of course, I don't need to tell you twice to make a function... or maybe I do. Make a function. Make a function. Make a function... alright, I hope you get the point. Now, honestly, this is the part that gets a bit tricky since we have to check if there are three in a row in any row, column, or diagonal. Let's look at each case by itself.

1. **Check Rows**

The simplest part to check who won is to check if there is a three in a row in any row of the board, and if a three in a row is found, we return true. For this, we use a for loop and then the **all()** function like this:

```
for row in board:
    if all(cell == player for cell in row)
        return True
```

Now, at this point, you are for sure wondering what this new function **all()** is. And honestly, I've been thinking of teaching you this function because it probably would've made both of our lives easier. Essentially, the **all()** function returns true if all elements in some **iterable** meet some condition (default is true, so all elements must be nonzero). In this loop above, the condition is if the cell is equal to the player (X or O), and the iterable in question is the cell variable looping across that row.

2. **Check Columns**

The second part to check in this winning function is whether there are three in a row in the columns, and if there are, we must return True. For this, we can again use the handy dandy **all()** function. Here is the code:

```
for col in range(3):
    if all(board[row][col] == player for row in range(3))
        return True
```

This is a bit more challenging, but it is still understandable, and you'll see how. The iterable, in this case, is the row that will be looping across a range from 0 to 3: 0, 1, 2. The condition, in this case, is just checking if all cells in a column are equal

page = page+1 # 109

to the current player. This might be a bit hard to wrap your head around, but it should be simple once we use this **all()** function more and more.

3. **Check Diagonals**

   The diagonals are the hardest ones by far. However, there are only two diagonals that we have to check, so either you can use a **for** loop, or you can just use a complicated **if** condition. What better way to improve your knowledge and practice than to purposely make things complicated? (This isn't a joke, by the way).

   The condition for the first diagonal can be done with something like this:

   ```
   all(board[i][i]) == player for i in range(3))
   ```

   And the condition for the second diagonal can be done with something like this:

   ```
   all(board[i][2 - i] == player for i in range(3))
   ```

   Putting it all together, we can have a condition like this:

   ```
   if <first condition> or <second condition>:
       return True
   ```

   And that's it for the diagonals!

Now, if none of these (rows, columns, diagonals) scenarios have produced a winner, then we return false, and we go to the next player's turn. However, not just yet, because though a winner is one way the game can end, we also have to check the other way, which is if the game board is all full. (I'm not even going to tell you when we need a function; you should just assume that it's a foregone conclusion).

To do this, we can use the godly **all()** function like this (really should've introduced it to you before, but what do I know):

```
all(cell != "-"for row in board for cell in row)
```

This is honestly a bit trickier than the other times we used **all()**. Because now the iterable is, in fact, a nested for loop. However, it still acts the same. You can also think of an **all()** statement like a for loop like this:

```
for row in board:
    for cell in row:
        if cell == "-"
            return False
return True
```

It really is the same thing as a **for** loop, but to be honest, nobody wants to type any more than they need to. And, plus, it still looks neat; it might actually be neater. With this out of the way, that finishes all the main steps, but before you read my amazing and uplifting conclusion (I never fail on that!), do some double-checks on your program. It's good practice, and you should always be safe rather than sorry. Also test out your program with your buddy, family member, your dog, or really anybody to see if it fully works. If it doesn't, just fix it and try it again!

But anyways, after everything is working (feel free to check solutions as well), that really does wrap up the Tic Tac Toe program, and I hope now you're starting to feel more and more comfortable with programming the more times we code and do this. I also hope that you are enjoying this because, trust me, reading some textbooks on how to code is much more tedious than this. I've tried it. I mean, why else would I go through all of this work, creating a book for other people, if I hadn't lived through that boredom myself? (No offense to anybody; every book I've read is still great!) But yeah, you should feel great doing this program, and honestly, you did that mostly by yourself, which is an amazing accomplishment! Though remember, in Kobe Bryant's words, job's *not finished, we still got work to do*!

Review:

- Plan and break the program into sub-tasks
- Use 2D lists
- Displaying 2D lists like a real tic-tac-toe
- Very handy – all() python function
- Traversing through 2D lists row-wise, column-wise, and diagonally

For GOATs: Expand the board to 5x5 and change the rules - now you need 4 in a row to win, and suddenly, every game becomes an epic showdown where even the first move matters way too much.

Wordle

How To Play

Guess the Wordle in 6 tries.

- Each guess must be a valid 5-letter word.
- The color of the tiles will change to show how close your guess was to the word.

Examples

W is in the word and in the correct spot.

I is in the word but in the wrong spot.

U is not in the word in any spot.

(Ref: https://www.nytimes.com/games/wordle)

If you knew how to spell during the quarantine in 2020, you probably know and played Wordle. I mean, this game had a bigger worldwide peak than Fortnite! It had adults and elderly people playing it like a ritual, making it a part of their daily routine. There is one issue with the entire "one word a day" process and that is… well, the one word a day. I feel like so many times I play Wordle and I'm just annoyed that there is only one word. Well, why not code it? We have all the computer power in our hands, and if we want (assuming you have no school), we can literally play all day.

Before we start coding, let's think about how the game works. Wordle is a word-guessing game where you have six attempts to guess a hidden five-letter word. After each guess, you get feedback on which letters are correct and in the right position (green), which letters are correct but in the wrong position (yellow), and which letters aren't in the word at all (gray). The goal is to guess the word before you run out of attempts. To build this, let's create our game plan:

1. Get a List of Words: We'll fetch a list of valid five-letter words from an external source.

2. Pick a Secret Word: We'll randomly select a word from the list for the player to guess.

3. Get Player Guesses: We'll ask the player to guess a word and validate their input.

4. Provide Feedback: We'll compare the player's guess to the secret word and give feedback using colored text.

5. Check for Completion: We'll end the game if the player guesses the word or runs out of attempts. Now, let's get into the nitty-gritty of each step.

First, we need a list of valid five-letter words. Instead of hardcoding a list (which would be boring and time-consuming), we'll fetch one from the internet. This is where the **requests** library comes in. The **requests** library is like a magical postman for your Python programs—it can fetch data from websites and bring it back to you. For example, in this scenario, we'll use it to download a list of words from the internet. For simplicity, I've already found a file on the internet for us: https://www-cs-faculty.stanford.edu/~knuth/sgb-words.txt

Now, here's how to get all the five letter words from the internet.

```python
import requests

def get_words():
    url = "https://www-cs-faculty.stanford.edu/~knuth/sgb-words.txt"
```

```
try:
    response = requests.get(url)
    words = response.text.splitlines()
    return words
except Exception as e:
    print(e)
    return []
```

The **requests.get(url)** function sends a request to the website and fetches the data. The **response.text.splitlines**() function splits the data into a list of words, one per line. But what is the try and except? Well, this ensures that if something goes wrong (e.g., no internet connection, or an error), we'll print an error message and return an empty list.

A **try-except** block in Python is like a safety net for your code. You put the code that might cause an error inside the **try** block, and if an error happens, the **except** block runs instead of crashing the program. It's a way to handle errors gracefully and keep your program running smoothly! Please refer to the Appendix for more information on how to use try/except block in Python.

Before moving on, this is the first time we're using external sourcing in this book, so let's talk about why it's so powerful. By fetching data from the internet, we can make our programs dynamic and up to date. For example, if the word list changes, our program will automatically use the new list without any changes to the code. It's like having a direct line to the internet—pretty cool, right?

Once we have the list of words, we'll have to randomly select one as the secret word. This is where the **random** library comes in. We've used it before, but this time, we'll use it to pick a word from the list. Here's the code:

```
secret_word = random.choice(words).upper()
```

As we know from before, the **random.choice**(words) function picks a random word from the list, and the **.upper()** function converts the word to uppercase for consistency. This ensures that the secret word is always in uppercase, making it easier to compare with the player's guess later.

Next, we need to let the player guess a word. We'll ask for their input and make sure it's valid. For example: *"Attempt 1 / 6: CRANE"*. Here's how we'll handle this:

```
guess = input(f"{Fore.RESET}Attempt {attempt} / {attempts}:
").strip().upper()
if len(guess) != word_length:
    print (f"Invalid word. The word must be exactly {word_length} letters
long.")
elif guess.lower() not in words:
    print ("Invalid word. The word must be a valid English word.")
```

The **input()** function asks the player to enter their guess, and the **.strip().upper()** function removes any extra spaces and convert the *guess* to uppercase. We then check if the *guess* is if right length and a valid word. If the *guess* is invalid, we ask the player to try again. This ensures that the player can only enter valid guesses, making the game fairer and fun.

At this point, you've probably noticed something funky in our code... and that is the **Fore.RESET**. Well, after each guess, Wordle gives feedback using colored text. This is where the **colorama** library comes in (remember, you must import it to be able to use it). **colorama** is like a magic paintbrush for your print statements—it lets you add colors to your text, making your programs look more polished and professional. Here's how we'll use it:

```python
feedback = ""
for i in range(word_length):
    if guess[i] == secret_word[i]:
        feedback += f"{Fore.LIGHTGREEN_EX}{guess[i]}"
    elif guess[i] in secret_word:
        feedback += f"{Fore.LIGHTYELLOW_EX}{guess[i]}"
    else:
        Feedback += f"{Fore.RESET}{guess[i]}"
```

The **Fore.LIGHTGREEN_EX** function makes the text bright green, indicating a correct letter in the correct position. The **Fore.LIGHTYELLOW_EX** function makes the text bright yellow, indicating a correct letter in the wrong position. The **Fore.RESET** function resets the text color to the default, indicating an incorrect letter. This feedback helps the player narrow down their guesses and improve their strategy.

colorama is a unique library because it works across different operating systems, so your colored text will look the same on Windows, macOS, and Linux. It's perfect for adding a little flair to your programs, whether you're highlighting important information or just making things look pretty. Finally, we need to check if the player has guessed the word or run out of attempts. Here's the code:

```python
if guess == secret_word:
    print (f"{Fore.RESET}Congratulations! You guessed the word!")
    print (f"{Fore.RESET}That was your last attempt! The word was
{secret_word}. Better luck next time!")
```

If the player guesses the word, we print a congratulatory message and end the game. If the player runs out of attempts, we reveal the secret word and encourage them to try again. This ensures that the game has a clear ending, whether the player wins or loses.

Review:

- Colorful display for the data
- Python module: **requests**
    - o Using requests.get method to send requests
    - o Using response.text and reponse.text to get data
- **colorama** Python module

For GOATs: Make your Wordle clone remember players by saving their stats between games - imagine knowing you've beaten your cousin 12 times in a row.

War

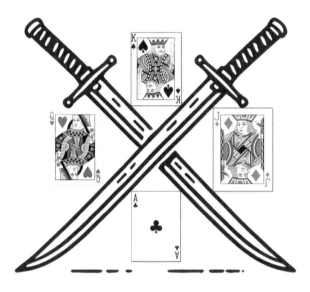

If I'm being completely honest, all the games and programs we've done so far in this chapter pale in comparison to the card game War. I mean, I've probably played this game for more hours than I've eaten food, and considering that I used to be a toddler, that's saying something. Like seriously, I remember many times when a friend and I would start a war game, and we wouldn't finish until days later. Although it is the most repetitive game ever, as far as I've thought of it, this game has all the elements we've learned in this entire chapter. It's perfect to conclude this part of the book!

At first thought, this game probably feels very overwhelming to code. Just thinking about it, you have to store yours and the computer's decks, the order, and ties, among many other parts of the game, and doing it with many functions would just get unorganized. But what else can we do in Python? Well, meet the **class**. No, not at all like the classes you have in school, nothing like that. I'm talking about a Python **class**, where a coder can use their full imagination to create anything they want!

A **class** is like a blueprint that can be expanded on to create different yet, at the core, very similar objects in Python. Now, actually, I just realized, I haven't taught you guys objects either. Objects in the real world are literally anything. They could be your laptop, a desk, or a chair, but what defines an object? Properties. Actions. And in Python, an object essentially has those two things. It has properties -- data that defines it, and actions -- functions that it can do. A very simple example of an object in Python is this list: [1, 2, 3]. It has data, and it can perform functions like **remove()**, which removes an element from the list.

Connecting this back to a class, you can create your own type of object that has properties and actions in the same way. Take a look at the syntax. I wrote a sample class below:

```python
class Character(object):
    def __init__(self, name, health, attack_power):
        self.name = name
        self.health = health
        self.attack_power = attack_power
    def attack(self):
        print (f"{self.name} does {self.attack_power} power!")
```

The first thing you probably notice is the strange **__init__** function... why is it named like that? Well, this is Python's way of starting a class. When creating a class, the computer calls this **__init__** function as a way of initializing the new object being created. The next thing you must look at is the **self**. The **self** is also probably a bit weird to you because you've obviously never used or created a **class** before. Essentially, self is a reference to the object itself... kind of like referring to yourself as "me" in real life.

The variables *self.name*, *self.health*, and *self.attack_power* are called instance variables. This means that these variables are unique and can only be used by the object (or instance) that it is a part of. Now, there is also another type of variable or property that you can create in a class, and these are called class variables. Class variables look like this:

```
class Character:
    species = "Human"
```

In this example, the species variable can only be accessed by functions in the class... but the difference is that it remains the same for all objects as it belongs to the class itself and can be accessed by all objects created using the class.

After the **__init__** function, we see an *attack()* function, also called **method**. The attack method contains the **self** object (which is itself; every function in a class must contain the **self** object in the parameter), and that's it. It uses that **self** object to print a statement to the console about the attack power. Now, methods of a class can only be called if an object is created. Let's take a look at how to actually create a Character instance.

```
warrior = Character("Warrior," 100, 15)
wizard = Character("Wizard", 80, 25)
warrior.attack()  # Output: Warrior does 15 power!
wizard.attack()  # Output: Wizard does 25 power!
```

We can see that the above statements create two characters: *warrior* and *wizard*, with different properties. Then, you can see an example of how to use/call a method. We must use period "." to tell the computer that it is a part of the object's class.

That's just a bit of the basics when dealing with classes. Of course, like anything in Python programming, and life in general, there's more to it, but you can either dig into that on your own time or wait until we talk about it later. But anyways, that's all you need to know for this program. Without further ado, let's get into the gameplan.

Now, why do we need a class for this program? Well, we have to keep track of the many complex variables that are used in the entire program and every function. However, by using classes, this organization and structure should become easier and better shaped. So why don't you take a look at what we need in this program and find out what classes we might need?

Well, since it's your first time coding with classes, I'll tell you what we need. We'll need, of course, a main class to call and initiate the actual game, a *Deck* class that can store all 52 cards, and a *Card* class that acts as a bare bone structure for all possible cards in the deck. Anyways, now that we know what classes to create, let's get into the gameplan for today!

1. Create Card, Deck classes
2. Create game class and variables
3. Create a game loop that asks user if they want to move on to the next round
4. Call round-winner function
   a. Get both user and computer card
   b. Find winner
   c. Call tie function
      i. Simulate "war"
5. Repeat game loop until winner is found

Well, I think we better get into the first step. There needs to be no further waiting, am I right? Let's start by creating the *Card* class, because we can't create a deck of cards without having cards. Now, in the *Card* class, let's first start with what properties we need. Well, we need a *suit* and a *rank*. However, we will also need one more thing, and that is the *rank as a number*. This is important because we will need an easy way to figure out what's higher between Jacks and Kings, or Queens and Aces, etc., and by using the corresponding number, the computer can easily do this. So, to accomplish this fact, I did this:

```python
class Card:
    suits = ["Hearts", "Diamonds", "Clubs", "Spades"]
    ranks = ["2", "3", "4", "5", "6", "7", "8", "9", "10", "Jack",
"Queen", "King", "Ace"]

    def __init__(self, rank, suit):
        self.rank = rank
        self.suit = suit
        self.value = self.ranks.index(rank)

    def __str__(self):
        return f"{self.rank} of {self.suit}"
```

Now, before I dive into exactly what I did, I want to mention the addition of the __str__ method, which probably confuses you. Though it looks like the __init__ function, it actually does a completely different thing. What it does is when a Card object is used in a print statement, it gets automatically converted to whatever the __str__() function returns. In other words, when you want to print the card, its __str__ gets invoked.

Anyways, getting to what I did, I essentially created a new property called *self.value* that uses a list and indexing (sorted rank list from 2 to Ace) to find a corresponding value. This way, Aces will be the highest-value card, and two will be the lowest-value card. And to be honest, everything else is pretty straightforward, given that you read and didn't just skip through the part I talked about in classes.

The next class that we'll have to make is the *Deck* class. Now, the Deck class is just 52 cards, which we can use the *Card* object to create all 52 different cards as a list. Using the *Card* class as a reference and some handy-dandy **for** loops, this should be pretty simple, so go ahead and give this your best shot. Don't forget to shuffle the deck (which we can do using a cool **random** function!) After creating the **__init__** function in the Deck class, we will also need to create a *deal* function within the class, because guys, what else would we use a deck for if it isn't to deal cards?

Now, to deal with this and make sure that we return the card at the very top or front of the deck list, I will introduce a function of Python's list object: **pop()**. Now, if the Deck list has an element in it, the **pop()** function will remove and return the first element of the list, which is exactly what we want to do... so I'll leave you to it to create that function. After you complete that little task, it's time to move on to the next step, which is to create the game class and game variables.

Now, like all the other classes and functions, you can name this game class however you want... actually, nope, you're probably going to name it completely irrelevant, like snowball or pumpkin. Frankly, I don't trust you guys, so I'm going to force you to use something plain: War. Now, in the **__init__** function for this class, we need to create the game variables. Well, to actually play the war game, we need to split the deck into two hands for each player. So, let's try doing something like this:

Now that we've correctly created (and remember to always test if your code is working) the game variables and the starting function for this class, we can move on to step three. What does step three say again... oh yeah, we have to create the game loop. So, for this, let's create a function that just contains the game loop. Now, the only thing I want to have in this loop is just a small input that asks if the user wants to move on to the next round, and if they do, we can just make a new function! That simulates another round! So, to do this, we can use, of course, not a **for** loop because no one knows when a full game of War will end, so we need a **while** loop.

Now, not only do we have to move to each round, we have to figure out when the game will actually end. And you know what this means! Another function! This function will check if the game has ended, which will happen if either the user or the computer has no cards in their hand. We can code that with simple conditional statements like below:

```
If not self.user_hand:
    return "Computer wins the game!"
elif not self.computer_hand:
    return "You win the game!"
return None
```

When creating these types of **if** conditions in functions, it's always good to make sure that if the game should continue (the previous two conditions don't work), then we must return **None** so the computer doesn't mess up the condition using the result. Anyways, now it's time to create the round winner function, which, if you've thought any of this was hard or complicated, you might be cooked (just kidding, I've got you).

I've already broken this function down into steps. So, in War, how do we find out the winner? We first have to get the cards from both the user's and the computer's hands. Now, to do that, we can again use the **pop()** function to get the first card in both hands. Remember to do *self.user_hand* and *self.computer_hand* and not just *user_hand* and *computer_hand*, since the **self** is really important. Also, remember that in all of this, using print statements to your advantage to make the console look good and make the user know what's going on in the game is also very important.

Getting back to the algorithm, now that we have both cards, we just have to check whose value is higher or if there is a tie. This can be done with simple **if** statements. Now, let's say the cards are different, and there is a definite round winner. In this case, both cards must be added to the winner's hand, and to do this, we can use the **append()** function of Python's list object.

```
def append(self, other_card):
    self.cards.append(other_card)
```

But what if the cards have the same value? Then what? Well, we can just look at what happens in real War when there's a tie... well, War!

Taking a break from the coding real quick, just so that we have the rules and are on the same page. When the cards are the same rank, three cards from each player are placed faced down. Then, a fourth card is pulled from their hand, and that is the new card that is being compared. If there is another tie, then there's another war, and so on. The war process ends when either there is a victory or when one person runs out of cards and cannot play the three faced down or doesn't have a fourth card.

And we just solved the first step of the coding puzzle. Really though, the hardest part of programming, which you'll learn when you become a CS person yourself (maybe, I actually don't know), is figuring out what to code and how to solve a problem. Once you know what to do, the coding part is actually the easiest... though I know it doesn't seem like that now.

So, the first step of this is to create two lists to keep track of what cards are from the user and from the computer. Of course, this starts with the original two cards that were played that were the same. Next, using a three-ranged for loop, we can get the next three cards that are faced down and add them to those piles. Remember to always use **if** conditions to check whether the hand has enough cards. Otherwise, the computer will give an error, which is something no young or old coder wants.

After that, it's time to get the fourth card from each hand. We can use similar **if** conditions as we did in the round winner function to compare both cards. Now, if the War is won, all cards from all piles must be transferred and appended to the winner's hand. However, you might be thinking, I can't append a list to a list (as if you tried it, there will be an error). Well, Python (and I) have the best thing for you! The **extend()** function! The extend function is literally the append function, but it appends multiple elements and takes a list as an input. So, stop whining; your problem is solved. Here is how you can write your extend method:

```
def extend(self, other_deck):
    self.cards.extend(other_deck.cards)
```

Now, if there's a tie again, which honestly is what we lived for when we used to religiously play this game, we have to call the *tie* function again and pass in the new user and computer pile that has the four cards added for each. Now, you might not believe it, but we are finally finished! Of course, we have to start the game class and call the start function, which I'll show you because I think you deserve it:

```
game = WarGame()
game.start_game()
```

Yeah, that's basically it, you finished the war game! And I can honestly tell you, this is a very complicated program, and it's probably up there for the most complicated program in the book, and that's saying something because we still have more waiting for you filled with new topics and vast ideas. So, this is the actual patting your back problem. I'm a bit hazy if I told you to pat your back for the first program in this chapter, Hangman, but this program should actually get a pat on the back. Honestly, go to your dad and mom and ask for a pat on the back; you deserve it. And actually... I probably deserve it. Writing this much to teach you guys is hard work, phew! But you are ⅔ of the way there! A great programmer in the making!

Review:

With the introduction of classes, I would say this is a step up to the next level of programming.

- Plan and break down a complex problem into smaller subtasks
- Introduction to Python classes
    - o Instantiating a class
    - o Methods and Attributes
    - o Class attributes

o   Accessing methods and attributes of an object

- Using class objects as members of another class

- More list functions: **pop**(), **append**(), **extend**()

 **For GOATs** Spice up the endless card battles by adding special abilities - make Aces trigger a "nuclear war" where both players burn 3 cards, or Jokers force a sudden death round.

Part 3: Diving Deeper

011: PRO

Alright, you've got functions down and built some solid games. Now, it's time to make your code do something truly useful. In this part, we're moving beyond the console and into the real world, where your programs will interact with websites, send emails, and solve problems that actually matter.

Here, you'll take everything you've learned to this point and put it into overburn. We're talking about using real live data from Wikipedia, as well as many other sources. And just when you think you've got it all figured out, we'll throw in the N-Queens puzzle, a chess problem that'll teach you recursion (we'll get into this in detail later).

But the most important thing (maybe other than recursion) is APIS. These are the hidden bridges that let programs talk to each other across the internet. Imagine typing one command and instantly fetching real sports scores, weather updates, or even latest trends... IN CODE. Trust me, once you see how easily your code can tap into the real world, you'll start looking at everything differently. And that's when you'll know, you're not just writing code, you're creating solutions.

What Happened on This Day

Have you ever woken up one morning and just thought to yourself: what happened last year today? What was my life like five years ago on this day? What about even further than that? And kept going on and on? I mean, I've always wondered what happened on this day. Even without asking, you must have gotten some notification from somewhere about something saying that some event happened on this day last year. Oh, that's it, Google Photos! They always remind you about this!

In all seriousness, though, you might be wondering…how in the world we can find out about an event that happened on this day. And you're wrong; there is no function that can do this in Python, but there are tools on the internet that we can use. Your mind should've thought back to how we used an online list of words for our Wordle program, but we actually won't be using that either. In fact, we'll be trying out something different this time, but it should open the possibilities to literally do whatever you like whenever you like. With this, you should truly understand the power of programming.

Meet APIs.

API stands for *Application Programming Interface.* But what is an API? Think of it like a waiter. It goes to one place, takes an order, goes to another, gives some food, goes to a third, takes an order again, etc. Essentially, a computer uses an API to request and receive data from a server running somewhere out there. To get the desired data, there are three simple steps that you need to take:

1. A program sends a request to an API

page = page+1 # 132

2. The API processes it and fetches needed data from a server

3. The API returns a response to the program (usually in a JSON format)

JSON (pronounced "jay-son") stands for JavaScript Object Notation. It's a way to store and organize information in a text format that's easy for both humans and computers to read. Think of it like a neatly labeled box where you can store things like names, numbers, or even lists.

Now, how do you send a request to the API? You issue a request like this:

GET https://api.weather.com/v3/weather?city=NewYork

First, the word "**GET**" indicates that you are requesting some information from the server. Next is the URL https://api.weather.com/v3/weather?city=NewYork. Now, what's a URL? It indicates the *address* where you can reach the server and what information you are requesting.

Then, the server responds with data (in JSON) to the above request:

```
{
    "city": "New York",
    "temperature": "22°C",
    "condition": "Cloudy
}
```

This, you might say, just looks like a Python dictionary, and you're absolutely right. This is the beauty of APIs in Python. The response can be immediately massaged into data that we can use right away. Now that you understand how we can use the APIs let's dig into the syntax of how to call them.

Just like how we used the **get()** function from the **requests** library to get a Wordle list, we will be using the library here but with a different URL. However, there is one difference. Instead of using **response.text**, we will be using **response.json**; I guess you know the reason why! That's it! But before we move on, here's a quick and easy example of using **requests** to call an API:

```
response = requests.get(url)
response_in_json = response.json()
```

Alright, now that you know the basics of using and calling an API, I think it's time to run you down for our game plan today.

1. Ask the user for month and day
2. Call the API to get the data
3. Display events

I know, I know, you're probably asking when looking at this game plan: dude, why is it so much smaller than Tic Tac Toe or War? Well, first off, I did tell you that War was probably the most complicated program here, and you are going to do most of it. Imagine it like I am helping you learn to ride the bike, and this is my way of slowly taking my hands off. Anyways, I think we should just get into it!

Now, we've been doing this for quite a while, just a simple input is needed for step number one. And remember, if you've taken a break as we move from chapter two to chapter three, functions, functions, functions. Always, all the time, you must use functions. Now, of course, for this input, we need to ask for the month and the day because that is the real basis of our entire program. In the last chapter, I didn't really tell you guys to validate these inputs, but as we move on to deeper topics, validation is key. So, in this case, how would we validate a certain input?

Well, for the month, the value that we get from the user must be between 01 and 12, and the day must be between 01 and 31 (in fact, this upper bound for the date differs based on the month). Now, if the input doesn't match these conditions, then the input must be taken again. These types of validation might seem tiresome, but they are very important in making sure nothing goes wrong, and every edge case is taken care of. Even without me reminding you guys, from now on, you must validate no matter what.

Anyways, let's move on to the second step, which is actually fetching the data. For this API, we will be using Wikipedia's *onthisday* feature. Here is the exact link we'll be using:

f"https://en.wikipedia.org/api/rest_v1/feed/onthisday/events/{month}/{day}"

Now, you might be wondering why we're using an f-string. Well, in this URL, we need to pass in the specified month and day, and because we have that information from the user, we can do something like the URL above. You can test it out yourself; just substitute the month and day with whatever you want and paste the link into the search bar. You'll actually get the data that we'll be using in the program. Pretty cool, right?

Anyways, look back to when I talked about the APIs before this program. You can really just use the same syntax to do this next step of getting the data from the API. Just make sure you use the **try** and **except** block so that no errors happen that break the entire program. Now, after this comes the biggest step of the program, though displaying doesn't seem like that big of a deal, and frankly, it really shouldn't be; it is the biggest part of this program!

Now, if you're trying to do this part by yourself, you might realize that you don't actually know how the JSON is structured. Since you didn't make the data yourself, you don't know how the keys and values are in the data, so what I always do in this situation is take a look at the data first. When you go to this URL on the Chrome browser, there will be a little check box that says "pretty-print". Click that button, and some of that huge mess of data will be cleaned up a little bit. You can also use the Firefox browser, which will neatly collapse all the JSON data for you.

When looking at all that data, you still might feel overwhelmed, as it should be the most data you've looked at in your entire programming career, but don't worry. Just take a look at it and try to navigate through using keys and values. For instance, we can clearly see now that all the real data is in the "events" key, so we can really shorten the data a lot by using that key. Then, in each event (which you can use a **for** loop for), there's a name and other details, so like that, you can try and find your way through the data. Of course, since it is your first time doing all of this, feel free to look at my answers and solutions. In fact, I'll include a tidbit of how I formatted everything below:

```
year = event.get("year", "Unknown Year")
text = event.get("text", "No description available.")
```

By using the **get**() function in the dictionary, I can easily either get the needed information or have a filler statement just in case that information isn't found. Once you've printed out all events and found some way of formatting them, you're pretty much finished! I know this program was a bit easy for the third chapter, but it's just a nice and simple way for you to be introduced to APIs, and you can't tell me you're not impressed. I mean, look at how easy it is to use real-world data! This is what it's all about! I promise you at the end of this chapter and at the end of this book, you'll have all the tools to start creating projects and programs using real data about whatever you want, but first, we have to get to the end!

Review:

You need to get out of your comfort zone if you want to excel in this section. But, with practice, all these things start clearing up. In this section, we learned how to talk to servers out there on the internet:

- Introduction to APIs
- JSON format
- Basics of different parts of requests: URL, get method
- Python module: **requests**
    - o Using **requests.get** method to send requests
    - o Using **response.text** and **response.json** to get data
- Sending requests to API servers
- Understand large JSON structures using browsers
- Parsing large JSON objects

For GOATs Explore other Wikipedia APIs,
https://en.wikipedia.org/api/rest_v1/
Get the information and send daily a mail with this to you and
your friends. Look for the next program on how to send emails.

Wikipedia Detective

Now that we know about how to access and use real data from the internet (APIs), let's look at others to play with. Alright! I've got an idea. Imagine you're a detective. But instead of solving crimes and putting away criminals, your job is to scour Wikipedia, figuring out which English words are the most important. Think of it like eavesdropping on someone's conversation, or in this case, a website. If you can find what words they are using the most, you can most likely understand what they are talking about, and the same applies to Wikipedia. What person would want to read an entire Wikipedia article when you can summarize it down to a couple of words?

Before diving into the actual code, how are we going to access Wikipedia data? I hinted at it before, and yes, we'll be using the Wikipedia API. To use it, we don't need to use any link since there is a built-in Python library for it: **Wikipedia-API.** To import it, do this:

```
import wikipediaapi
```

Just like the Wordle program, the library might not exist for you, so you can:

- Go to settings -> Project -> Python Interpreter
- Search for **Wikipedia-API**
- Install the package

But if you're on a MacBook, there will likely be another error, but it won't occur until you run the finished program. If you're worried about this now, just run the same program and:

- Go to finder -> Applications -> Python
- Run ./Install Certificates.command

Hopefully, this will help, and the program will run as expected!
Now, I think it's time to make a game plan for this program.

1. Get user input for Wikipedia article name and article
2. Clean up the article
3. Get word counts from the article
4. Plot frequency graph

Before looking at step 1, we must gather our imports, which is really step 0 in all these programs. For this, we will need six imports:

```
import wikipediaapi
import re
import nltk
import matplotlib.pyplot as plt
from collections import Counter
from nltk.corpus import stopwords
```

To be completely honest, you don't need to know what a lot of these imports do; just know that they are vital to the program…otherwise, why would we import them? Anyways, the first thing to do is to get the article we want to look over from the user; we can do this using simple inputs. Once we have the article name, we must get the real article and store it in a variable, and this is where the API comes in.

```
def get_wikipedia_text(article_title):
    """ Fetches content of a Wikipedia article."""
    wiki = wikipediaapi.Wikipedia(user_agent='GOAT Coder',
language='en')
    page = wiki.page(article_title)
    if not page.exists():
        print("Article not found!")
        return None
    return page.text
```

When we instantiate the Wikipedia class, it will establish a connection to Wikipedia API. Then, we are free to search through it to find the article our user wants us to eavesdrop on.

Of course, if the page doesn't exist, we cannot do much about that, but if it does, we must store it.

Now that we have the article (if we don't have, we'll just end the program right there), we have to clean it up. What do I mean by that? Well, we need to separate all the words from the various punctuation that might be in the article. Since we only care about words, we want to get the article boiled down into a list of plain words.

```python
def cleaner(text):
    """ Removes punctuation, converts to lowercase, and splits words."""
    text = re.sub(r'[^a-zA-Z\s]', '', text.lower()) # Remove punctuation
    words = text.split()     # Split into words
    return words
```

At first glance, you might see that I'm using **re.sub**(). If you think back that far, we have actually used this before in both our English to Pirate and Gen Alpha to Parent programs. In the same way, instead of replacing punctuation with some other word, we just want to delete it...so we will replace it with an empty string. But what is that jumble of letters? Well, that is actually an expression that tells the computer to substitute anything that isn't a letter. If you want to learn more about what each part of the expression means, I recommend searching up regular expressions, in short, **regex**.

The next step in this program is to filter the words. If we were real detectives, eavesdropping on someone's conversation, we wouldn't want to note how many times they say words like "the" or "it" because they don't mean anything. Instead, we only want to focus on words like names, actions, etc.

```python
def filter_words(word_list):
    """ Removes common stopwords and very short words."""
    stop_words = set(stopwords.words("english"))
    filtered = []
    for word in word_list:
        if word not in stop_words and len(word) > 2:
            filtered.append(word)
    return filtered
```

Instead of manually creating a list of words we want to ignore, why not let the computer do it? In the **nltk.corpus** library, there is already an object called **stopwords**, that will help us here. All we need is to create a simple **for** loop, and voila! We have finally massaged and gotten the data we need. Now, we just need to get the proper frequencies of all the words remaining, and for this...you guessed it. Another built-in function.

```python
word_counts = Counter(filtered_words)
```

For this, we are using the **Counter** class from the **collections** library. This function literally outputs the counts for each element in a list, which is what we need. At this point, now that we have our results, we need to display them in a reasonable form. And for that, I think it's best if we use a graph.

```python
def plot_word_frequency(word_counts):
    """ Plots the top 10 most frequent words."""
    top_words = word_counts.most_common(10)
    words, counts = zip(*top_words)
    plt.figure(figsize=(10, 5))
    plt.bar(words, counts, color="blue")
    plt.xlabel("Words")
    plt.ylabel("Frequency")
    plt.title("Top Words in Wikipedia Article")
```

```
plt.xticks(rotation=45)
plt.show()
```

In Python, the library to plot a graph is **matplotlib**, and it is actually famous for being the main library that can actually create images and plots. It's fairly straightforward, as most of the code just labels axes and changes different settings. Play around with these settings and see how the graph changes accordingly. Once this code is done, the program should work correctly! Now, you have your very own Wikipedia detective. This gives you a way to save time, as now you don't need to read an entire article; rather, you can just look at what words are being used to infer what the key points are.

Now, before you start using this for all your schoolwork and start telling your friends about how easy everything is, I'd actually keep this on the low. I'm not trying to be the reason your teacher gets mad when this entire detective operation blows right back at you. But anyway, I really hope you can see the power of coding now that we're using real data and creating projects that have real use cases. If that's all, then adios!

Review:

In this section, we explored various other Python modules and how to use them to our needs:

- Splitting complex problems into smaller tasks
- Installing Python modules in PyCharm
- Python module **wikipediaapi**: to access Wikipedia articles
- Python module **matplotlib.pyplot**: to plot graphs
- Using **stopwords** object from Python module: **nltk.corpus**: to get common English words
- Using Python class **Counter** from the **collections** module
- How to massage text using different string functions and functions from **re**

 **For GOATs:** Turn your article analyzer into a bias detector by comparing how often positive vs. negative words appear in political articles.

Email Sender

Let's be real: when I said I'd teach you how to make real-world progams at the start of this book, I wasn't talking about translators and minigames. Nope, I was talking about power. Imagine that you're a club president and you've promised to send your members a good morning email daily. But, just like everyone else on the planet, you love sleeping and hate waking up early. That's where this program comes in handy. Using this, you can send emails without the click of a button, and who knows, the possibilities of this are endless!

Before I give you guys our game plan for this program, we first must talk about how we can actually connect with a Gmail account and send an email. To send an email like this in Python, we have to use a library called **smtplib**. This library just makes it very easy for us to send emails using the Simple Mail Transfer Protocol (SMTP), which essentially just handles and creates a connection to the email server and sending process. I am not really going into the inner workings of SMTP here in this book. If you want to dive into that topic, feel free to have a 30-minute session on your own to learn more about it.

Now, with that, I think I've given you enough reasons for you guys to understand how powerful this program really is, so without any further speculation from parents or the FBI or whatnot, let's dive into the game plan.

1. Imports
2. Configure all the details
3. Create an SMTP server connection
4. Create email message
5. Set up the server

6. Print Statements

The first step in this program is importing the right libraries, and for this, you need to import three things, which I will list below:

```
import smtplib
from email.mime.text import MIMEText
from email.mime.multipart import MIMEMultipart
```

We've already talked about **smtplib**. The second import is used to create a text message. The third import is to create an email body that can take both text and also other types, let's say, a picture or a video or audio clip of your favorite song that you want to send across. We'll be using all three of these later in the program.

Now, getting to the second step in all of this which is honestly the most important, because if you don't do it correctly, the whole program will break. In your Python code, you must have variables containing your email, password for that, and the recipient's email. That isn't enough if you are using a newer update for Gmail (which everyone and their grandmother are using). You will get an error if you use your regular Google account password. This is because Google actually has a security in place that protects third-party programs from signing in using SMTP.

By the way, you're lucky I had to do all of this before you because this fix took some time. Anyways, to fix this, you must follow these steps below:

1. Go to your Google account ("Manage your Google account")
2. On the top, click the search bar
3. Search "App passwords"

4. Under "App Name", write Gmail

5. Copy your app password and use that in your variable instead of your Google account password

If you've followed these steps to a tee, the future error in Google's security won't be an issue. In fact, this is Google's fix to this problem since it still allows third-party apps to connect to Google's account. So that leads us to step number three, which is to create the SMTP server. To do this, we have to write this code:

```
smtp_server = "smtp.gmail.com"
smtp_port = 587
```

Now, the reason we need to do this is because this is Gmail's SMTP server. The port number must be 587 because that is the one used if you want to have a secure connection to the Gmail server, and no bad actor can snoop into your messages. This step was pretty simple, and now we can move on to step number four, where we actually create the message we want to send.

Before we do this, we have to figure out some minor things like how many emails we want to send (change the range in the **for** loop), and we have to, like all the requests and internet-related things we've done, use a **try** and **except** statement. Now, here is the code to create the object that will have the details of our email:

```
message = MIMEMultipart()
message["From"] = sender_email
message["To"] = recipient_email
message["Subject"] = f"Test Email..."
```

This is pretty straightforward, as the "From" must be the sender's email, the "To" must be the recipient's email, and the "Subject" is just whatever subject the email will be. Of course, I just used placeholders in my solution on GitHub, but you can feel free to write your soul out to whomever you send your email to.

Within this step, we also must create the text of the email, and for that, we use the **MIMEText** function. For example, you can do something like this:

```
body = f"This is a test email"
message.attach(MIMEText(body, "plain"))
```

This code snippet just creates a plain text section and adds it to the message variable, which contains all of our other email data. This concludes the actual data that must be gathered to send the email, and for step five, we set up our own SMTP server to send the message across. To do this, we must use these four lines of code:

```
with smtplib.SMTP(smtp_server, smtp_port) as server:
    server.starttls()
    server.login(sender_email, sender_password)
    server.sendmail(sender_email, recipient_email, message.as_string())
```

This piece of code is probably the most complicated and weird-looking snippet you've laid your eyes on to this point, but if you take it line-by-line, it's really not that complex. Honestly, because it is Python code, you can probably figure out what the code does, but I'll make it even easier for you.

Essentially, the SMTP function establishes the connection of our program to the SMTP server. Next, the **starttls** function starts the TLS encryption. The next line is to log in with the specific credentials that we gave it, and lastly, it actually sends the email using the details we gave it: the to, from, and message content.

Now, after this is done, we can give a success or fail message in our **try-except** block. Of course, in the **except** block, we need to give our failure statement, indicating the error occurred. However, outside of the **except** block, we know that the program was a success, so after printing this, we can truly celebrate! Wait, wait! Try attaching a picture when you try it out. Hint: Use MIMEImage.

Now, before just moving on to trying it out on your friends, if I were you, I would test it out using your parents emails. Also, try sending them things from your sibling. Once your parents find out, I promise you it will give them a laugh of a lifetime! Once that works, you're free to try it with all your friends.

But remember, if you try and send like a thousand or even a million emails to a friend or your teacher or something, don't blame me if you get in trouble at school or your email gets banned... just don't do those things! But anyways, this is just another cool step on our Python programming journey, and I'll see you in the next program! Peace!

Review:
A fun program simulating an email client that shows how to send emails:
- Using Python module **email.mime.text**
- Creating a message using the **MimeText** class
- Creating multipart messages using **MimeMultiPart**
- Creating SMTP server
- Sending emails using your Gmail account

 **For GOATs** Write a scheduler program in Python that sends you a good morning e-mail with a random Wikipedia page. It's a fun way to start your day with some learning. You can extend it by sending daily reminders for an important upcoming test. The possibilities are endless.

Upcoming Sports Events

Before I even get into this, you can basically figure out what this program is going to do just based on the title. In this program, I am going to get more in-depth into APIs, and it's really just a step up from the *What Happened on This Day* program. So, if you don't like sports, you should still tag along, and I guarantee that at least someone in your family or someone you know enjoys watching sports and making this program will help them out big time!

Now, getting into it, have you ever felt that feeling of missing out on your favorite sports team game last night? You can't believe you missed it...you were probably busy or just forgot (of course, it was a great game, too!) Either way, you now have to dodge spoilers, scroll through any of the highlights, and pretend you watched the game and know what happened when talking with your friends. I mean, it's just a horrible situation, right? (I know I'm exaggerating, but just play on with it.)

But what if there was a way where you would never miss a game? Do you always know when the next game is with only a click of a button? Well, that's the beauty of coding and APIs for you! No more frantic Google searches and missed games; you're ready to become that all-watching sports fan! Without further ado, let's get into how exactly we will be coding this program.

First, we need to find a free API online to use so that we can get all the data about different games for all the different sports. Luckily for you, I've already found one: **api-sports.io**. Now, if you want to do more of this type of stuff, like getting sports data and player stats and doing cool projects with that, here's a little bit to know about **api-sports.io**. It's essentially a service that provides a large variety of sports data, making it very simple for programmers like you to access live scores, upcoming games, player stats, and more. And the very big thing is that… it's free! When you move on to more advanced APIs in programming, you will come to learn that many of these high-powered services are actually paid…and let me tell you right now: it ain't cheap.

The second thing we have to do before starting to code is to set up the API. Unlike the **wikipediaapi**, which we used last time, we have to do a couple of things first before using this API. To just keep it brief and simple, here are the steps to set this API up:

1. Log in to https://api-sports.io/ (either with Google or through the website)
2. On the left, there should be a sidebar where you should click on Apis
3. Now, you will see a bunch of sports (I'll be using basketball for this program). Click on the sport for which you want to find upcoming games.
4. In the dropdown menu, click on live demo.
5. Here, you will use two things
   a. Under the **endpoint**, you will see a weird-looking link. This is the **host link**: it tells the computer where to fetch the data
   b. Under the **host link**, you will see the API KEY. This key is kind of like your password so that the service knows that you are authorized to access the data. Each person has a different API key.

Now that you've done these steps (and really, it probably wasn't that hard) and taken note of the *host link* and the *API key*, you should be ready to go! But wait… what about the actual link that we'll be using to make a request in Python? Well, if you want to take that challenge of finding the actual link, look into the documentation that **api-sports** gives you.

page = page+1 # 153

It should be in the dropdown menu for whatever sport you choose. So, either you can do it the hard way, which you probably should, or use the link I used. Again, keep in mind that the link I used was for basketball.

f"https://v2.nba.api-sports.io/games?date={date}"

As you can see, I've used the host link, and by using an **f-string**, I can easily feed it the date on which I want to see upcoming games. Anyways, now that we have the API key and URL, we can move on to the gameplan.

1. Create API headers
2. Send the request
3. Get response data from the server
4. Iterate through games and get needed data
    a. Teams
    b. Time
    c. Arena details
    d. Status of the game (in progress, completed, etc.)
5. Display games

At first glance, this game plan seems quite simple, and that's because it is just the API headers that include the API key and a URL containing the real date from the user.

```
url = f"https://v2.nba.api-sports.io/games?date={date}"
headers = {
      'x-rapidapi-key': <your api key>,
      'x-rapidapi-host': 'v2.nba.api-sports.io'
}
upcoming_sports(url, headers)
```

When following and copying this code snippet, everything must be exact. The keys for headers must be *x-rapidapi-key* and *x-rapidapi-host* because the server can only understand these headers. And, of course, the *date* variable is found by using input from the user. Next, we must actually turn this pre-data into real results using the Python **requests** library.

```
response = requests.request("GET", url, headers=headers)
data = response.json()
```

If you can recollect, we've actually done this before. Essentially, we use the **requests** module to send a message to the API, asking it for some data. The API key is needed because the API itself needs to make sure we aren't some suspicious parties. After getting back the response data, this is where the program will kind of split off. In our API from **api-sports**, all the data is organized differently for each sport: different dictionary names, different keys, and different values. This means that I can't actually give you a working code for whatever sport you want (unless it's NBA, since I'm doing that too).

However, there's no need to worry because it's simple to figure out the structure of the data. First, run your program in debug mode and stop it at the line where you get response data. From here, PyCharm makes it easy to navigate through the debugger, and like this, you can create the code to find all the details of the game. For example, I'm using the NBA API, so here is my code.

```
games = data['response']
for game in games:
    game_id = game['id']
    home_team = game['teams']['home']['name']
    visitor_team = game['teams']['visitors']['name']
```

```
game_time = game['date']['start']
status = game['status']['long']
arena_name = game['arena']['name']
arena_city = game['arena']['city']
arena_state = game['arena']['state']
```

After you've gotten all your data (and if you are still struggling, just follow along with the NBA API), it's time to display this to the user, who is patiently waiting for information. To do this, either you can print out all the games after this for loop, or you can print a game one by one inside the for loop. There is really no big difference between them, but you can do whatever you want.

Once you've completed that, we've successfully finished another program! If you're a sports lover like me, I'll probably use this more than I use my phone. Well, that might be a stretch, but still – it'll be very useful. Now, if you're not a sports lover, I guarantee you learned something out of this and are starting to get the hang of all this API and massaging real data. Well, I think that will do it for this section, and we got past that so easily I don't even think a break is needed! #On to the next!

Review:

This section shows more ways to collect data from the internet:

- Using Python **requests** module
- Using API Keys to authenticate

 **For GOATs:** Connect this to a ticket API to find the cheapest seats because real GOATs don't just track games - they scheme how to attend them.

N-Queens

Have you ever played chess? You probably have. Now, have you ever had more than one queen on board? Again, if you know how to play and have played before, chances are that you have, of course, by promoting a pawn. But have you ever, in a real game, had three queens on the same board? Four queens? Eight queens? I can guarantee that you haven't, but that's the problem that we're going to explore for this program! Of course, it isn't realistic, and I know that's the promise I made to you guys at the start of the book, but stay with me now.

The N-Queens problem is actually very well-known in the coding community and in math. Essentially, you have to place some N number of queens on an N-by-N chess board so that no queen is in line of sight and can kill another. This can be very hard to do just by using our brains, as the queen can travel across and around the entire board wherever it is placed. Now, by this time of the book, you probably know where this is going: we're going to code this and figure out a solution…and you're right! But how would it be fair to you not to experience the struggle of this game when using a real chessboard? So, why don't you take a break right now, go find a chess board, use some number (eight is the hardest), and try and find a way to place all queens without any of them being able to capture each other? Take your time, and it's okay if you don't find one.

Now that you've taken that short break let's talk about how to solve this problem. Now, when dealing with these more complex problems (let's face it, this is much harder than any problem from before), it's natural to first find out how to solve it in the easiest way possible. So, to find this, how would you try to solve this? What strategy would you use in your placements?

Well, if I were to manually place queens until I find a problem, I would do it in two options. The first option would just be to randomly check every single combination of queens on the board in no particular order. After placing the queens on the board, I would just check if two queens are in a position to capture each other, and if they are, the position is invalid. Now, there is one big problem with coding and, honestly, manually doing this. First, I want you to try to figure that out.

Well, like a human or real-life form, some actions take time. Yes, even computers take time, though much less than humans! Until now, we haven't had to deal with this; our code always takes little to no time at all. But this problem is different. Let's say we are taking N = 8, so we need to safely place eight queens in an eight-by-eight chess board. If we were randomly checking every combination of placements, how long would it take? How many combinations would we have to check?

Well, if you know combinations and permutations, this is a simple math problem…the answer is 8 factorial or 8 x 7 x 6 x 5 x 4 x 3 x 2 x 1, which is equal to around 2.6 million combinations. Now, for the computer, which I'll get into more depth soon, this actually isn't that much, but as N increases, you can see that these 2.6 million combinations will increase rapidly!

Okay. Now we know that this strategy, though simple, will not work and is not efficient for the computer to do. So, what's another strategy? I would just pick placements in a systematic manner, checking every single combination, starting with a queen at A1 on the chess board.

For example, if I was solving it with N = 4, I would place my first queen at A1, then check the next row for which squares I can place my second queen. I would then see that the only squares I can place my queen on the second row are B3 or B4. Looking at the two options, I would first try B3; however, the third row would not have any possible "safe" spot for my third queen. Because the specific position of the first two queens does not work, I would then shift the second queen to the next possible position, which is B4. Now, in the third row, the only safe spot for a queen is C2. I would then check the last row, which, in this scenario, doesn't have any spots left. I would then repeat what I did with the second row and backtrack. Now, in this case, I would have to backtrack all the way to my first queen at A1. This means that I would now start with A2 instead of A1.

page = page+1 # 160

In the coding world, these types of problems can be solved by the technique called **recursion**. To explain it simply, **recursion** happens when a function repeatedly calls itself, breaking down the big problem into smaller jobs until it reaches a base case. Let's look at the easiest use case for **recursion**: the *Fibonacci*! If you've never looked at the *Fibonacci* numbers in math class, you're in for it now. The *Fibonacci* sequence is just an infinite list of numbers where the next number in the sequence is the sum of the previous two. Here's how the first ten numbers of the sequence:

0, 1, 1, 2, 3, 5, 8, 13, 21, 34

Now, how does recursion apply to this? Well, we must figure out how we can break down the task of finding the nth *Fibonacci* number into smaller parts. Since we know each number is the sum of the previous two numbers, we can repeatedly create smaller tasks. Let's say we are tasked with finding the 5th Fibonacci number. Look at the diagram below to find out how **recursion** works:

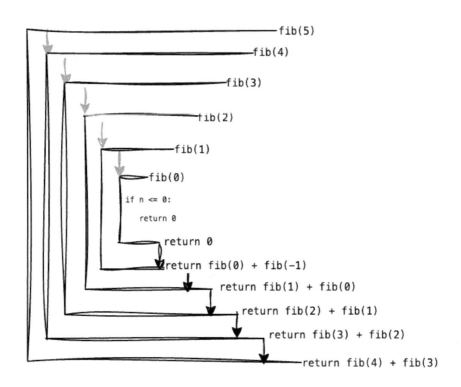

Hopefully, this diagram explains how we can use recursion to split big problems into smaller ones. To implement this in code, take a look at this:

```python
def fibonacci(n):
    if n <= 0:
        return 0
    return fibonacci(n - 1) + fibonacci(n - 2)
```

As you can see, recursion isn't really that difficult. In code, it's just calling the same function inside of itself but giving smaller tasks and problems. In this case, every time we call the *fibonacci* function, the task is split into two parts: finding the previous number and finding the second previous number.

Well, now that we're on the same page about recursion and have come up with how to solve this problem, it's time to code it! So, here is the game plan:

1. Create a function to be called recursively
   a. Check for a safe spot for the given row
   b. Do recursion for the next row
   c. Backtrack and try the next safe spot
   d. Repeat and break when there are no more safe spots
2. Create a board for each solution
3. Print Solutions

The first order of business is to create the main solving loop. Most of the time, when using recursion, there needs to be a main function involved. This is because recursion requires some setup before and data collection after. The problem is when calling the same function over and over in an act of recursion, you are very limited to things you can do that don't affect the actual recursion.

In this first function, we need to create the initial empty board. Now, instead of creating a 2D array with all elements as an empty string, I thought it was best to just have a 1D array filled with –1. This is because when going through all the rows during recursion, we can just assume that the index of the list is the row and set the value to the column since we know there must be one queen per row. Also, in this first bit, we need to call the recursive function.

Before looking into the recursive function, let's look at its heading and parameters:

```
def place_queens(board, row, n, solutions):
```

This is important as we have to determine how to change the parameters to actually create smaller problems for the computer. In this case, we will just need to keep adding one to the row: row + 1. However, the first thing needed in any recursive function is the base case. The base case in this scenario is quite simple: when the row reaches n, we know we have a solution in the making.

```
if row == n:
    solutions.append(create_board(board, n))
    return
```

When we know we have a solution, we need to actually create the 2d board from our 1d board/row list. To do this, we can create another function.

```
def create_board(board, n):
    solved_board = []
    for r in range(n):
        solved_board.append("")
        for c in range(n):
            if board[r] == c:
                solved_board[r] += "Q"
            else:
                solved_board[r] += "."
    return solved_board
```

Though this function looks very complex, we can see that it is just using the queen placements in the 1d array to find the corresponding queen cells. The rest is filled with blank cells. After implementing the base case, it's time to create the logic of the algorithm we talked about beforehand. The first step in our plan is to check the current row for a safe spot, which I believe requires another function.

```
def is_safe(board, row, col):
    for r in range(row):
        c = board[r]
        if c == col or abs(row - r) == abs(col - c):
            return False
    return True
```

In this function, we are going through all the queens previously placed and comparing them with our current (r, c) cell. In the first part of the **if** condition, we are checking if a previous queen has the same column, which if it's true, means this cell isn't safe. In the second part of the condition, we are checking if any previous queen is on the same diagonal as our selected cell. Note that we don't have to check for the same row because our queens will always be on separate rows. After creating the function, here is how we'll use it.

```
for col in range(n):
    if is_safe(board, row, col):
        board[row] = col
        place_queens(board, row + 1, n, solutions)
        board[row] = -1
```

After checking if the current cell is safe, we can then temporarily add that to the 1d board list. Then, we can recursively call the function with the change being the next row (row + 1). Now, assuming that it all works out, when that path has been completed, regardless of whether a solution was made or not, it is time to backtrack. This is the most important step in the process because to backtrack; we need to make it seem like nothing ever changed in the 1d board list. To do this, all we have to do is change the value from col back to –1.

Once you have coded that step, we will finish the recursion! All we have to do now is print the solutions, and eureka! The program and your first recursion are completed. If you want to make sure your code is working, try changing the n value to different numbers. Then, validate the program's solutions by getting a chessboard and physically checking it out. Does it work? If it doesn't work, what changes do you have to make? Now, I can't help out every person individually, but you can use the correct solution on GitHub. And with that subtle reminder, I think I'm done for the day. Sayonara!

Review:

A popular N-Queens chess program showcasing the power of computers:

- Introduction to Recursion
- Fibonacci program showing recursion in the works!
- Brainstorming different ways to solve N-Queens
- Using recursion to solve N-Queens

For GOATs: Find all possible solutions for N-Queens and plot them using matplotlib. Solve the N-Queens problem with boards of different sizes (mxn). Introduce obstacles to make it more interesting.

Whiskers' Hunt

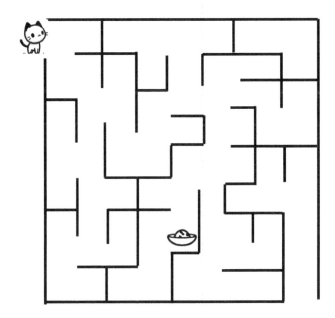

Alright, imagine this: you have a cat named Whiskers, and like all cats, Whiskers is both curious and easily distracted by food. One day, Whiskers wanders into a maze, and somewhere inside this maze, there's a delicious bowl of cat food. But there's a problem— Whiskers has no idea how to get there!

Lucky for Whiskers, you are a genius programmer who can use an algorithm called Depth-First Search (DFS) to help the cat find its way. But first, how does this work?

Let's think like a cat for a second. Whiskers doesn't know the **best** way to the food, so the plan is to try a path, follow it as far as possible, and if it leads to a dead-end, backtrack and try a different way.

This is exactly how **Depth-First Search (DFS)** works! The algorithm follows a path as deep as it can go, and if it gets stuck, it backtracks and tries another option. So, now that we understand the algorithm let's take a look at the game plan.

1. Setting up the Maze

2. Finding Whiskers' Starting Point

3. Using DFS to Search for Food:

    a. Looks in four directions (right, left, down, up).

    b. If the next move leads to an **open space or food**, it continues moving forward.

    c. If Whiskers reaches the food, we stop!

    d. If Whiskers hits a dead-end (a wall or a visited spot), it **backtracks** and tries a different path.

4. Marking the Path

5. Printing the Final Maze

The first step in this program is to actually create the maze. Now, for the sake of simplicity, I have manually created a maze that we can use for our little experiment. The maze follows different symbols:

- **C** is where Whiskers starts.
- **F** is where the food is waiting.
- **#** represents walls that Whiskers cannot walk through.
- " "(empty spaces) are paths Whiskers can take.

```
maze = [
    ["#", "#", "#", "#", "#", "#", "#", "#"],
    ["#", "C"," "," ", "#"," ", "F", "#"],
    ["#", "#", "#", " ", "#", " ", "#", "#"],
    ["#"," "," "," "," "," "," ", "#"],
```

```
        ["#", "#", "#", "#", "#", "#", "#", "#"]
]

# Directions: Right, Left, Down, Up
moves = [(0, 1), (0, -1), (1, 0), (-1, 0)]
```

Not only that, but I initiated a list that contains all possible moves Whisker can take: right, left, down, and up. For example, the right move corresponds to (0, 1), as Whiskers' column must increase by one. In the same manner, the left move corresponds to (0, -1), as Whiskers' column would decrease by one.

The next step is to actually find Whiskers' start position. Even though we manually created a maze, we still need to have the computer find the initial starting point. This is because if you ever replace the manually created maze with a random computer-created one, you will need a portion of the program to find Whiskers' starting point.

```
# Find the start position
for i in range(len(maze)):
    for j in range(len(maze[0])):
        if maze[i][j] == "C":  # "C" is the cat
            start = (i, j)
```

As you can see in the code snippet above, all we need for this is a simple nested for loop and a condition that checks if the current cell is "C". After finding Whiskers' start, we can now move on to the bulk of the program: the DFS. Just like our N-queens program, we need to start off with our base case.

```
if maze[x][y] == "F":
    print("\nWhiskers found the food!")
    return True
```

In this scenario, our base case is when the current cell has the food (F). If Whiskers reaches the food, we stop the DFS and print out the board. But if this base case is not true, we must get on with our recursion. The first thing that must be done whenever visiting a new cell is to mark it with a paw print (in our program, we are using ".").

```
maze[x][y] = "."    # Mark as visited (cat's paw prints)
path.append((x, y))
```

Keep in mind that we have to update both the actual 2d array, maze and the actual path list. After doing this, we have to look for the next move, which could be any of either right, left, up, or down. Lucky for us, we already have the additives in a list we made prior.

```
for dx, dy in moves:
    nx, ny = x + dx, y + dy
    if maze[nx][ny] in (" ", "F"):   # Move if it's an open space or food
        if dfs(maze, nx, ny, path):
            return True
    path.pop()
```

For every possible move, we first check if it is either an open space or a food space. If it's not either of those (wall or visited), then there's no point in going to that space. But if it is, then we can start to explore using DFS in that new cell, which is why we call the function then. The last part of this snippet is very important. Just like N-queens, backtracking is vital to the program, and in this case, we are using the **pop**() function. The **pop**() function just deletes the last item in a list, which in this case would be the last added cell.

Once the recursion function has finished and found a proper path through the maze that goes from starting point to finish, it's time to print. For this, we can use simple for loops to first update the maze board and then print it like so:

```python
for x, y in path:
    maze[x][y] = "*"

print ("\nFinal Maze:")

for row in maze:
    print (" ".join(row))
```

Once you've typed the last bit of this code snippet, you are finished! Your imaginary pet cat, Whiskers, is now able to find the food that it has patiently waited for. Give yourself a pat on the back because you just saved a cat's life!

This simple program sneaks in an important concept—how computers explore possibilities when solving a problem. Just like Whiskers doesn't know the best path ahead of time, a computer doesn't either. It just follows a set of logical rules to explore paths and find a solution. So next time you're lost (whether in a video game or in real life), just remember: think like DFS! Try one way, go as far as you can, and if it doesn't work, backtrack and try another path. Who knew that a lost cat could teach you how to think like a programmer?

 **For GOATs:** Explore other pathfinding algorithms like A* (https://en.wikipedia.org/wiki/A*_search_algorithm) and see the difference in pathfinding time between dfs vs A*

Part 4: AI

At this point of time, you've built games, automated tasks, and made your code talk to the internet. Now it's time for AI, where we teach computers to learn patterns and make their own decisions (and hopefully not take over the world... yet). Here's the truth: AI isn't some black box that only geniuses understand. It's just a bit of math wrapped in code, and you're about to unwrap it!

We'll start with a simple linear regression, which teaches the computer how to predict future outcomes based on past data. Then we'll move on to clustering, where the computer will group similar things atuomatically. However, the real showstopper is image recognition. In this part, you'll build a system that can tell the difference between cats and dogs. We'll use real libraries, but don't worry, we'll keep the math to a minimum and focus on real stuff you can use.

The coolest part about all this is that these aren't just abstract concepts. That linear regression model could predict your next game's high scores. The same clustering algorithm could organize your music playlist by mood. And the image recognition could be perfect for sorting through your massive camera roll or screenshots folder. Overall, this is where our coding transforms from giving computers instructions, to them teaching themselves how to learn.

Basics of AI

So, what is Artificial Intelligence (AI)? You can think of AI as another person, capable of doing many things like us, yet still consisting of wires and computers. At least, that's what we think it will be in the near future. It's still in the early stages of learning, but it has shown promise in many areas. I mean, we're living in a world with self-driving cars...soon, we won't even need a driver's license!

Now, if AI is all about computers doing tasks like humans, what is machine learning about? Well, machine learning is actually a subsection of AI, and it is all about how computers use past data to make future decisions. Many techniques have been invented over the years for efficient machine learning, and we'll get into more depth in just a bit. For now, let's look at some real-world examples for both AI and ML.

Assume that you're struggling to solve math problems on your study guide and stressing out because you have a test the next day. Instead of freaking out, what if you had an AI-powered helper (in fact, there are apps like this already!). All you have to do is take a picture of your problem, and the app will give you a step-by-step solution. Now, how does this relate to AI? Well, the computer must first understand the handwriting of the problem statement – a human process. Then, it has to look at past problems to find a way to solve them correctly, which is a human process. From this, we can see that AI can be used in many scenarios.

Now, let's look at an example of ML. As a high or middle schooler, you probably listen to music...a lot. Maybe you use Spotify, Apple Music, YouTube Music, or whatever, but you always need to know when the next album is dropping, what the latest hits are, etc. Now, one thing in common with all these different apps is that they all have a cool recommendation system in place. But how does the recommendation system work? Well, the computer tries to find patterns in what you listen to (e.g., genre, artist, etc.), which gives you new songs based on that. As you can see, this is a form of machine learning, and if you look closely, you'll start to uncover many more things that use ML as well.

A specific model or technique that computers use in ML is neural networks. You might have heard this term in your biology or science class. In science, a neural network refers to the interconnected map of neurons in the brain. In computer science, it refers to a technique used to teach the computer that mimics the human brain. But mimicking the human brain is easier said than done, so how is this possible?

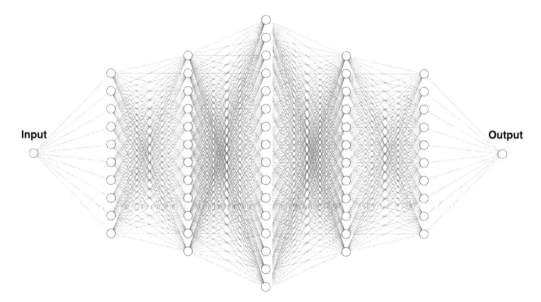

A neural network is just a map of artificial neurons that work together to process and produce information...and it does this using layers. The first layer is where the data is input; it could be a grainy photo of an apple, a random number sequence, etc. This data then goes through many "hidden" layers, where the computer tries to find patterns, recognize features, and learn. Finally, the last layer outputs the result; it could be identifying an object in an image or predicting the next number in a sequence. At first glance, all of this might not make too much sense, but there are many resources online that can help you understand more.

Linear Regression

Linear Regression is the first project and algorithm you need to know in machine learning. Linear Regression is a tool used by scientists and computers that takes past data into account and, in return, spouts a prediction. For example, let's say your parents tell you that more sleep equals better test scores, but you want to experiment with that. Before each test (though I'm not sure why anyone would risk their scores), you slept for a different amount of time and recorded it in this table.

Hours of Sleep	Test Scores Max:100
10	92
8	88
6	79
7	78
9	84
4	68

Just by looking at the numbers (or by plotting them on a graph), you can see that the test scores increase as the hours of sleep go up. But how do you predict the test score for any given number of sleep hours? Well, to manually do Linear Regression, you have to draw a best-fit line, which is an infinitely long straight line drawn to show the exact correlation. For example, the line might look something like this:

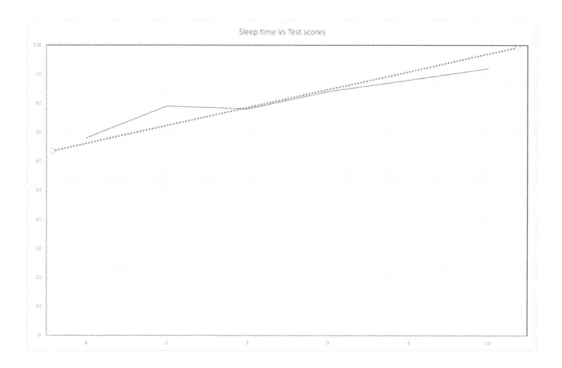

This is where the magic happens! As you can see, when the x-coordinate is at 10 (if you take 10 hours of sleep before the test), the y-coordinate is at 92, which is the prediction. It takes the previous values and data, finds a best-fit line, and uses that line to predict. You might think it doesn't take a genius to figure this out...but guess what? Sir Francis Galton has something to say about it.

Like this example, I think it's easy to see the scope where Linear Regression can be used. In more significant issues, it can predict house prices, stock markets, college acceptance, and many more. So now let's look at how we can use Python to implement Linear Regression.

Before we code, though, if we're trying to predict something, we need to get actual data. To find these large datasets, you can visit Kaggle.com or data.gov. These websites have hundreds of thousands of datasets that people have already made and shared with the public. I picked a WNBA dataset, where I'll try to predict the amount of wins a team has based on their stats. Of course, you can try to predict something completely different, and trust me, it gets addicting!

The first thing to do when you get the data set (make sure to unzip the file) is to add it to your workspace by uploading it. Not only that, but we have to read the data and store it in a variable. Don't worry too much about the code, but here is how we do that:

```python
import pandas as pd
import numpy as np
import matplotlib.pyplot as plt
from sklearn.model_selection import train_test_split

df = pd.read_csv('/content/teamstats.csv')
```

By the way, yes, all the imports are needed. Getting back to it, since we only have one dataset, we must split the dataset into two. Why? Well, we need a training dataset so that the Linear Regression model can create a line of best fit and find the correlation, and we need a test dataset to see if our model is predicting well. Most of the time, when splitting, we need a much more extensive training dataset because we want the Linear Regression to take into account a lot of data.

```python
train, test = train_test_split(df, test_size = 0.2, random_state = 0)
X_train = train[[col for col in train.columns if col in ['ppg', 'oreb']]]
y_train = train[['w']]
```

```
x_test = test[[col for col in test.columns if col in ['ppg', 'oreb']]]
y_test = test[['w']]
```

The first line of the code snippet above splits the dataset into train and test. However, we can't just start there. In my example, I want to see if points per game and offensive rebounds are good predictors of winning games. This is why, in both the *x_train* and *x_test* variables, I am only taking into account those two columns. The *y_train* and *y_test* variables only keep the wins column, which is what we are going to measure our predictions against.

Now that we've set everything up, there's nothing left but to create the Linear Regression model.

```
from sklearn.metrics import mean_squared_error
from sklearn.linear_model import LinearRegression

reg = LinearRegression().fit(x_train, y_train)
reg.predict(x_test)
```

When coding this, it is very important that you use both *x_train* and *y_train* as parameters because these datasets have the most data. After running this code snippet, you will most likely get a list of numbers. This list of numbers is your prediction for all entries in the *x_test* dataset, and to check, all you need to do is print the *x_test* dataset, and voila! Now you can see how well the linear regression model worked out! If you aren't happy with your results or just want to change your predictors (mine were ppg and oreb), I encourage you to keep changing until you find the best predictors.

Clustering

Another technique that is used for pattern recognition within ML is clustering. Imagine you're on the college admissions team. You must go through a giant pile of student applications, but you're way too lazy to read them one by one. But what if there was a way to quickly sort all the applications into groups like these:

- The Superstars: 4.0 GPA, insane SAT scores, probably the next Einstein.
- The Averages: Decent grades, decent SAT, they live a balanced life.
- The Carefrees: Didn't work much, but hey, at least they tried...?

I'm sure it's easy for you to think about how much time would be saved if the applications were split into these groups. And lucky for all college admissions teams and you, meet K-Means Clustering! In simple terms, K-Means clustering is an algorithm in which the computer splits up data into K groups by randomly picking data observations as group "leaders". Here are the steps in this technique:

1. Decide how many groups you want (K)
2. Randomly pick K data observations as group leaders
3. Assign every other data observation to the leader they are closest to
4. Find the center observation of each group – now the new group leader
5. Reassign observations to the new groups
6. Repeat until observations do not switch after reassigning

Again, like Linear Regression, this might seem a bit confusing at first, but just think about it as a way to group data effectively. And now, there's nothing else to do but code!

page = page+1 # 182

The first step is to create or get real data. To keep it the same as the college admissions analogy I gave you at the start, I think it'll be best if we create our own data. However, we can't just use any list because the already-made **KMeans** function does not take that data type. This is why we must use **numpy** arrays like this:

```python
import numpy as np
import matplotlib.pyplot as plt
from sklearn.cluster import KMeans


# Sample data: (SAT Score, GPA, Extracurricular Score out of 10)
students = np.array([
    [1550, 4.0, 9],    # Top applicant
    [1480, 3.9, 8],
    [1200, 3.2, 6],    # Average applicant
    [1250, 3.3, 5],
    [980, 2.5, 3],     # At-risk applicant
    [1020, 2.8, 2],
])
```

As you can see, I've made a 2D array, storing the SAT score in the 0th index, their GPA in the 1st index, and a rating of how well their extracurriculars are on a scale from one to ten. I have seven data observations in my dataset, but of course, you're welcome to add as many as you want. The next step is to apply **K-means** and fit it to our dataset.

```python
# Apply K-Means Clustering (3 groups)
kmeans = KMeans(n_clusters=3, random_state=42, n_init=10)
kmeans.fit(students)
labels = kmeans.labels_
centers = kmeans.cluster_centers_
```

The code above does just that. It uses the built-in KMeans function and fits it to the dataset that we just created that stores the students' data. As you can see, we are also storing the final three centers in the K-Means clustering, and that leads us to the next step: plotting. To actually see and visualize our results, that is where the **matplotlib** library comes in. This library is very famous in Python because it is the most used visualizer and grapher out there. For simplicity, though, we don't have to go into depth on it.

```python
# Plot results
fig = plt.figure(figsize=(8, 6))
ax = fig.add_subplot(111, projection='3d')
ax.scatter(students[:, 0], students[:, 1], students[:, 2], c=labels,
cmap='coolwarm', edgecolors='black', s=100)
ax.scatter(centers[:, 0], centers[:, 1], centers[:, 2], c='yellow',
marker='X', s=200, label="Centers")
ax.set_xlabel("SAT Score")
ax.set_ylabel("GPA")
ax.set_zlabel("Extracurricular Score")
ax.set_title("College Admissions Clustering")
ax.legend()
plt.show()
```

The above code correctly graphs the clusters in a very descriptive way. Most of this code is quite straightforward. You can change the color of the graph, change the label names, the size of the points, etc. But I'm sure you're not worried about that. You're probably thinking to yourself, what in the world does this graph mean?

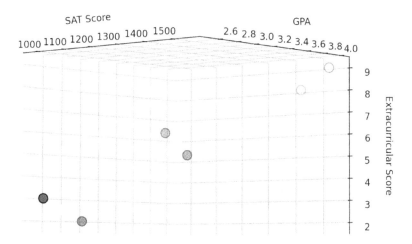

College Admissions Clustering

Well, let's first talk about the high-level and legend. The dots each represent a data point. Each dot is a different color depending on what cluster they are in. The yellow X's that are seemingly in the middle of each cluster are the true centers, representing the average student for each group. Now, what does cluster mean, though? Well, in this case, since we picked K = 3, it will create three groups of students using all predictors/columns. For example, depending on our dataset, these three groups that encompass all observations could be

1. High SAT, high GPA, and strong extracurriculars
2. Low SAT, low GPA, but strong extracurriculars
3. High SAT, weak extracurriculars

These groups will change based on how your dataset is, but hopefully, this experiment has shown you the creativity and ideas that can be made using clustering with K-Means. If you want, I highly recommend you take a real dataset, like we did with Linear Regression, and turn it into a number of clusters. You could also try to find the number of clusters (K) that receive the best results!

Image Recognition

Have you ever tried finding pictures of your friend in your camera roll? Sometimes these pictures are easy to find, but sometimes they aren't. That's why many photos apps created features where you can search for different people... but how does that work? How does the phone/computer know how your friend looks like, and navigate through all pictures to find them? That's where image recognition and classification comes in handy.

Image recognition and classification are two of the most important parts of AI-driven software. This is because not only can it be used for fun and silly reasons (like finding pictures of your friend), but it can also be used for global issues like identifying diseases early, detecting fraud, and even catching criminals more easily. Going into more depth, let's take the example of wildfires. If you live in the US, you know that over the past couple of years, wildfires have been increasing rapidly in size and frequency.

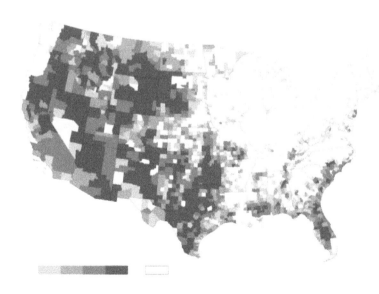

Looking at this graph above, you can see that this has become a very serious problem. Though we have very good and quality first responders, they cannot do everything. Also, news is spread much after the start of the fire, leading to more consequences. But what if we had cameras? What if, in those cameras, was a fire-detecting AI? I believe that would make it much easier to control fires before they become too big, and in fact, I'll be teaching you how to use an AI to do just this.

In computer science and AI, to create an efficient image classifier model, you must use neural networks. At the start of this chapter, I talked about them a little bit, but to refresh, it's just a computer technique or system that mimics how a human brain makes connections, and it works in a series of layers. We'll be using a specific type of neural network: the CNN (Convolutional Neural Network). The main difference between this and the normal neural network is that the CNN has different layers for different sections of the supposed image. Instead of connecting all portions of the image and looking at it, it splits it up and finds patterns within.

In Python, there are a couple of main libraries that allow us to do that, but we'll use TensorFlow. Again, if you want to know and research more about this library and see what more it can do, go for it! But if you're good, I think it's time to get into the code.

The first order of business is to just set up the rest of the program.

```python
import tensorflow as tf
from tensorflow.keras.preprocessing import image
import numpy as np
import ssl

ssl._create_default_https_context = ssl._create_unverified_context
```

Not only do we have to import, but we also have to make sure the CNN will be downloadable. Normally, the computer needs to check if whatever we are downloading or getting from an outside source is safe. The line above just tells the computer in advance not to check its safety and to trust the user (us). After this precaution is taken care of, the next step is to actually load in the model that we're going to be using, which is called MobileNetV2.

```
model = tf.keras.applications.MobileNetV2(weights='imagenet')
```

Again, throughout these programs in this chapter, a lot of the code can be ignored and not thought of too much. This is because the important part is to understand the concepts, as much of the code to implement the concepts comes from various advanced libraries. After actually getting your hands on the model, it's time to pick our test image. Honestly, for this, you can just surf the internet, save an image, and plop it into your PyCharm workspace. Once you do all of that, you can put this code.

```
img_path = "shirt.jpeg"
img = image.load_img(img_path, target_size=(224, 224))
img_array = image.img_to_array(img)
img_array = np.expand_dims(img_array, axis=0)
img_array =
tf.keras.applications.mobilenet_v2.preprocess_input(img_array)
```

In this code, all we are doing is taking that image from the internet and processing it in a way that can be used by our CNN model. This processing includes resizing, converting formats, and applying transformations like rotation or flipping.

Now, after doing all of this, we still have to get the results, and our CNN will give a list. This list will have all the different objects that it thinks are relevant to the image and cool enough; it will also give confidence in each one.

```
predictions = model.predict(img_array)
```

Now, we can do one of two things with these results. Either we can just forget about everything except the top-n most confident items, or we can display the entire thing. My vote is to just simplify this and display the top three. We can do this by using a **for** loop and **print** statements, and I know you've been craving for some regular keywords!

```
decoded_predictions =
tf.keras.applications.mobilenet_v2.decode_predictions(predictions,
top=3)[0]


# Print top predictions
for i, (imagenet_id, label, score) in enumerate(decoded_predictions):
    print(f"{i + 1}: {label} ({score * 100:.2f}%)")
```

And once that's done, great! You've created your very own image recognizer. Like this, try using simple images, complicated images, images with multiple subjects in frame, etc. Have some fun messing around with this AI model before moving on. This is where the strength of AI really shows, and I know that even with the simple knowledge you have gained on this, you can make something incredible.

Part 5: Achieving GOAT Status

Hey! Look how far you've come. Remember when printing "Hello World" felt like an accomplishment? Now you're building real projects that have real implications. But here's the thing: being a truly great coder isn't just about knowing how to code. It's also about how you think, solve problems, and work with others. In this final section, I want to share the stuff nobody really teaches you. The real-world skills that make the difference between someone who can write code, and someone who can build with it.

We'll talk about how to write code that is pleasant to read and work with (your future self will always thank you), how to debug, and how to organize bigger projects so that they don't turn into a big mess. But it's not just about the technical stuff. We'll also talk about developing your own coding style. For example, you will have to answer questions like: Should you always go for the fanciest solution? When is it better to keep things simple? And more.

The coolest part is that you will get to decide what coder you want to be. Maybe you want to make a living off of solving complex algorithms. Maybe you like creating video games. Whatever path you choose, I promise these tips will help you to grow exponentially. Finally, this isn't the end of your coding journey – it's the beginning of doing it like a pro. All this learning has given you the skills. Now let's talk about how to use them like a GOAT.

Write Code Like a Pro

The difference between a beginner and an expert programmer is not just solving problems but solving them in a clean, optimized, and readable way.

1. **Code Quality: Write Clean, Maintainable Code**
   - Bad code might work once, but great code works forever.
   - Follow best practices: indent properly, avoid redundant code, use functions effectively, and structure your project well.
   - Use meaningful variable and function names instead of generic ones like x and y.
   - Example of bad vs. good code:

   Bad code:

   ```python
   def                                              c(x,y):
       return x**y
   ```

   A few days later, you won't remember what this does.

   Good code:

   ```python
   def calculate_power(base, exponent):
       """ Returns the base raised to the power of the exponent."""
       return base ** exponent
   ```

   Notice a clear function name and a short comment explaining the function.

2. **Writing Edge Cases & Test Cases: Make Sure Your Code Never Breaks**
   - Great programmers think like hackers—they try to break their own code before someone else does.
   - Always test edge cases - empty inputs, negative numbers, and very large numbers.
   - Use assert statements and unit testing frameworks like **unittest** or **pytest**.
   - For example,

   ```python
   def divide(a, b):
       if b == 0:
           raise ValueError("Cannot divide by zero")
       return a / b


   try:
       divide(5, 0)
   except ValueError:
       print("Edge case passed: Cannot divide by zero")
   ```

```
# Test cases
assert divide(10, 2) == 5
assert divide(-4, 2) == -2
assert divide(5, 1) == 5
```

3. **Optimization: Make Your Code Fast and Efficient**
   - A slow program is a useless program. Learn to optimize your code by reducing time and space complexity.
   - Learn Big O Notation to understand how fast your code runs.
   - Always ask yourself:
     - o Can I do this in fewer steps?
     - o Can I use a better algorithm?
     - o Can I store results to avoid repeating work? (Memorization)
   - Example of optimization:

   Inefficient solution (O(n^2), slow):

```
# Finding duplicates in O(n^2)
arr = [1, 2, 3, 4, 2, 5]
for i in range(len(arr)):
    for j in range(i+1, len(arr)):
        if arr[i] == arr[j]:
            print( "Duplicate:", arr[i])
```

   Optimized solution (O(n), fast):

```
# Using a set for fast lookup
arr = [1, 2, 3, 4, 2, 5]
seen = set()
for num in arr:
    if num in seen:
        print ("Duplicate:", num)
    seen.add(num)
```

4. **Readability & Comments: Write Code That Others Can Understand**
   - Code is read more than it is written. Make sure others (or you in the future) can understand it.
   - Use comments only where necessary.

- For example:

```
def factorial(n):
    """
    Calculates the factorial of a number using recursion.
    Example: factorial(5) = 5 * 4 * 3 * 2 * 1 = 120
    """
    if n == 0 or n == 1:
        return 1
    return n * factorial(n - 1)
```

5. **Choose the Right Data Structures**
   - Lists, sets, dictionaries, trees, and graphs all serve different purposes.
   - Choosing the right data structure can make your code **faster and more memory-efficient**.
   - Example of using the right structure:

   Bad: Searching for an item in a list (O(n), slow)

```
names = ["Alice", "Bob", "Charlie"]
if "Charlie" in names:
    print("Found!")
```

   Good: Using a set for fast lookup (O(1), fast)

```
names_set = {"Alice", "Bob", "Charlie"}
if "Charlie" in names_set:
    print("Found!")
```

Explore Paths to Mastery

1. **Competitive Programming (USACO, Codeforces, Leetcode)**
   - Teaches you to think fast, write efficient algorithms, and debug quickly.
   - Start with USACO Bronze, then move to USACO Gold.
   - Solve problems on Codeforces, Leetcode, and AtCoder.
   - USACO Guide: https://usaco.guide/
   - Codeforces: https://codeforces.com/

2. **Contribute to Open Source**
   - Work on real-world projects and collaborate with other developers.
   - Find beginner-friendly projects on GitHub and start contributing.
   - Best beginner-friendly repositories: https://firsttimersonly.com/

3. **Build Passion Projects**
   - Nothing beats hands-on experience.
   - Some project ideas:
     - A personal finance tracker
     - A web scraper for movie ratings
     - A basic AI chatbot

4. **Build Passion Projects**
   - AI tools like ChatGPT and GitHub Copilot can boost productivity but don't just copy-paste answers.
   - Use AI for debugging, refactoring, and learning better coding patterns.

Master the Industry Skills

If you want to be better than 99% of programmers, you need to know more than just coding. Learn:

- Version Control (Git & GitHub)
- Linux & Shell Scripting
- Databases (SQL, NoSQL)
- Cloud Computing (AWS, Google Cloud, Azure)
- Web Development & APIs

Final Words: Becoming the Best Takes Time

The best programmers didn't become great overnight.

- Write code every day.

page = page+1 # 195

- Challenge yourself with difficult problems.
- Build projects that excite you.

If you follow this roadmap, you won't just be a "good" programmer—you'll be THE GOAT.

Appendix

1. **What are libraries? Why do we need to import? How to import?**

   Imagine you're working on a big project, like building a treehouse. You have some tools, but you realize you need a few special ones—like a power drill or a level—to get the job done. Instead of making these tools yourself, you can borrow them from a friend's toolbox. In Python, these toolboxes are called libraries, and they're filled with pre-built tools (code) that can help you solve problems or add cool features to your project.

   When you want to use one of these tools, you first need to bring the toolbox into your workspace. This is called importing. For example, if you need math tools, you'd write import math. Now, you have access to all the tools in the math toolbox, like calculating square roots or working with numbers.

   But what if your friend doesn't have the toolbox you need? No problem! You can get it from a store called PyPI (Python Package Index) using a tool called pip. For example, if you need a toolbox for working with websites, you'd type pip install requests in your command prompt. Once it's downloaded, you can import it into your project and start using it. If you are using PyCharm or any other visual editor, you can download the libraries as shown in this picture.

Sometimes, you don't need the whole toolbox—just one tool. In that case, you can borrow just that tool. For example, if you only need the square root function from the math toolbox, you'd write from math import sqrt. Now, you can use sqrt directly without needing to reference the whole toolbox.

Note: If you ever get an SSL error when trying to install a Python package or make a web request, just remember: Python is trying to be safe, but it needs permission to access Mac's certificates. Running ./Install Certificates.command is like giving Python the keys to the internet—so it can securely connect without any drama. You can go to the Applications folder on Mac, find your Python installation folder, and run the Install Certificates.command script.

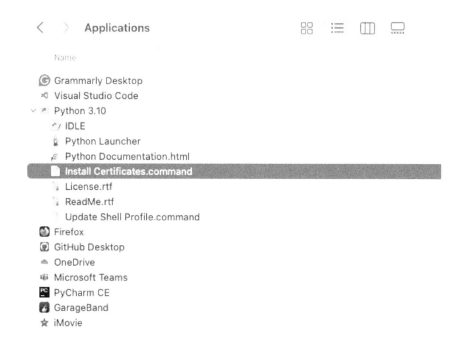

Applications

Name

- Grammarly Desktop
- Visual Studio Code
- Python 3.10
  - IDLE
  - Python Launcher
  - Python Documentation.html
  - **Install Certificates.command**
  - License.rtf
  - ReadMe.rtf
  - Update Shell Profile.command
- Firefox
- GitHub Desktop
- OneDrive
- Microsoft Teams
- PyCharm CE
- GarageBand
- iMovie

2. **What is a Try-Except Block?**

In Python, a **try-except block** is like a safety net for your code. It helps you handle errors gracefully so your program doesn't crash when something unexpected happens. Here's how it works:

Try Block: You put the code that might cause an error inside the try block.

Except Block: If an error occurs, the code inside the except block runs instead of crashing the program.

3. **Why Use Try-Except?**

Imagine you're playing a video game, and suddenly, the game crashes because of a small mistake. That's no fun, right? Try-except blocks are like a "game over" screen that lets you retry instead of crashing. They help your program keep running even if something goes wrong.

Example 1: Division by Zero

Let's say you're writing a program to divide two numbers. What if the user tries to divide by zero? That would cause an error. Here's how you can handle it:

```
try:
    numerator = int(input("Enter the numerator: "))
    denominator = int(input("Enter the denominator: "))
    result = numerator/denominator
    print(f"The result is: {result}")
except ZeroDivisionError:
 print("Oops! You can't divide by zero. Please try again.")
```

What Happens:

- If the user enters 0 for the denominator, the program will print:

  Oops! You can't divide by zero. Please try again.

- If the user enters valid numbers, the program will print the result.

Example 2: Invalid Input (Non-Number)

What if the user types something that's not a number? Let's handle that too:

```
try:
    numerator = int(input("Enter the numerator: "))
    denominator = int(input("Enter the denominator: "))
    result = numerator/denominator
    print(f"The result is: {result}")
except ZeroDivisionError:
    print("Oops! You can't divide by zero. Please try again.")
except ValueError:
    print("Oops! That's not a valid number. Please enter numbers
only.")
```

What Happens:

- If the user enters 0 for the denominator, it catches the ZeroDivisionError.

- If the user enters something like "hello", it catches the ValueError.

Example 3: Catching All Errors

Sometimes, you might not know what kind of error will happen. You can use a "catch-all" except block to handle any error:

```python
try:
    number = int(input("Enter a number: "))
    print (f"You entered: {number}")
except:
    print ("Oops! Something went wrong. Please try again.")
```

What Happens:
- If the user enters something invalid (like a word instead of a number), the

  program will print:

  Oops! Something went wrong. Please try again.

4. **Key Points to Remember:**

   Try Block: Put the code that might cause an error here.

   Except Block: Handle the error here so your program doesn't crash.

   Specific Errors: You can catch specific errors like ZeroDivisionError, ValueError, or FileNotFoundError.

   Catch-All: Use a generic except block to catch any error, but be careful—it can hide bugs!

5. **Why is Try-Expect Useful?**

- It makes your programs more user-friendly by handling mistakes gracefully.

- It prevents your program from crashing unexpectedly.

- It helps you debug by showing clear error messages.

About the Author

Aryan Poduri is a high school student with a deep passion for computer science and artificial intelligence and a hobby in digital art. From solving coding challenges to creating digital graphics, Aryan loves blending creativity with technology. In fact, he personally designed all the graphics—including the cover—for this book. Beyond his own projects, Aryan finds joy in helping middle and high school students explore the world of coding, making it more accessible and exciting for everyone. Whether through writing, teaching, or creating, he hopes to inspire others to see coding not as an intimidating skill but as a powerful tool for innovation.

When he's not coding, Aryan enjoys playing basketball, pushing himself on the court just as he does in his programming challenges. He also has a passion for snowboarding, carving through fresh powder, and tackling new slopes. Whether it's debugging code or perfecting a jump on the mountain, Aryan believes that persistence and creativity are the keys to mastering any skill.

Aryan's curiosity goes beyond coding and sports—he loves finding connections between different fields, like AI and language or tech and human behavior. Whether he's tackling a tough coding problem, researching a new idea, or competing in USACO and DECA, he thrives on challenges that push him to think in new ways.

More than anything, Aryan sees learning as an adventure. From building projects like his sports-focused app, Votopolo, to helping others code, he's always looking for ways to create and inspire. To him, coding isn't just about writing lines of text—it's about solving problems, expressing creativity, and making an impact.